W9-AED-159

THE MAN WHO FLEW

CHURCHILL

BRUCE WEST

THE MAN
WHO FLEW
CHURCHILL

BRUCE WEST

McGRAW-HILL RYERSON LIMITED

Toronto   Montreal   New York   London
Sydney   Mexico   Panama   Sao Paulo
Johannesburg   Düsseldorf   New Delhi
Singapore   Kuala Lumpur   Auckland

920

Vanderkloot, W. J.

The Man Who Flew Churchill

ISBN 0-07-077757-8

1 2 3 4 5 6 7 8 9 10 D 75 4 3 2 1 0 9 8 7 6 5

Printed and bound in Canada

Prologue

I believe that ever since man, but recently conscious of his own existence, saw the birds, he has desired to emulate them. Among the myths and fables of every race are tales of human flight. The paradise of most religions is reached through the air, and through the air many gods and prophets have passed from earth to their respective heavens; and all authentic angels are endowed with wings.

—Sir Arthur Whitten Brown, who with Sir John Alcock accomplished the first nonstop airplane flight across the Atlantic Ocean on June 15, 1919.

The success of Captain Alcock and Lieutenant Brown, while proving, not for the first time, that they are very gallant men, does not, it must be confessed, prove much else . . . .

As far as can be foreseen, the future of air transport over the Atlantic is not for the aeroplane. It may be used many times for personal feats of daring. But to make the aeroplane safe enough for business use on such sea routes we should have to have all the cyclones of the Atlantic marked on the chart, and their progress marked in from hour to hour . . . .

—The *Manchester Guardian,* June 16, 1919.

Although Alcock and Brown made the first nonstop flight across the Atlantic, they missed by two weeks the glory of making the first aerial crossing of that wide and dangerous sea. This triumph went to a huge flying boat of the United States Navy designated as the *NC-4* (*N* for Navy, *C* for Curtiss and *4* for the order of its emergence from the production line).

The aerial assault of the U.S. Navy upon the formidable Atlantic was, for its time, an extremely elaborate and well-organized enterprise. For one thing, it was to utilize four of the big four-engined flying boats, each weighing 28,000 pounds, having a wingspan of 126 feet, a fuel capacity of 1,610 gallons and carrying a crew of six. Along the entire projected trans-Atlantic route from a base at Far Rockaway, Long Island, N.Y.; to Trepassey Bay, Newfoundland; to the Azores; to Lisbon, Portugal; to Plymouth, England, there had been deployed no less than sixty U.S. naval vessels of various sizes, spaced at regular intervals to help provide directional information to the aircraft and, if need be, to act as rescue ships in the event of forced landings at sea.

Before the flight could get underway, the *NC-2* was removed from the running when it was severely damaged by fire in its hangar. The three remaining machines—*NC-1*, *NC-3* and *NC-4*—departed from Far Rockaway on the 1,000-mile hop to Trepassey Bay on May 6, 1919, at 10.00 A.M. *NC-1* and *NC-3* completed the nonstop flight without trouble in twelve hours. *NC-4* was not so fortunate. No sooner had it put Long Island behind it than one of its engines lost oil pressure and had to be switched off. Two hours later, a second engine snapped a connecting rod and *NC-4* had to make a forced landing in the sea eight miles off Cape Cod. Wallowing in the ocean all night as it taxied on the rough surface with the aid of its two remaining 400-h.p. Liberty engines, the *NC-4* eventually reached the U.S. Naval Air Station at Chatham, where the damaged engine was changed. The aircraft then continued on to Newfoundland with a stop at Halifax, Nova Scotia. At Trepassey Bay, the *NC-4* developed more engine trouble and the power plants had to be replaced. Her frustrated captain, Lieutenant-Commander A. C. Read, had no way of knowing then that in this particular venture the last indeed would be first, as the rather curious old adage maintains.

On the morning of May 16, a few minutes after six o'clock, the three flying boats took off from Trepassey

Bay for the Azores. During the flight they would not try to remain in formation. Each would make its way alone. Using Newfoundland as the jumping-off place for the overseas journey because of its relative proximity to the coast of Europe, the event was to be the first of a long series of successful and unsuccessful attempts to fly the Atlantic.

By the morning of May 17, the *NC-3*, hopelessly lost in miserable flying weather, had to land on savagely rough seas. The crew was rescued by the S.S. *Ionia* but the battered aircraft sank after an attempt was made to tow it.

The *NC-1* did somewhat better. It continued to fly on throughout the night and for several hours into daylight before it too became lost in dense fog and had to land on the sea about 100 miles west of Flores Island, part of the Azores group. The seas were running twenty feet high. But by May 18, the *NC-1* had managed to taxi across the wildly tossing surface of the Atlantic to the island of Ponta Delgada. Its crew proudly spurned during the last few miles, an offer of assistance from the U.S.S. *Harding* which had finally located the downed flying boat and had come racing to its aid. But the *NC-3* was, by this time, too damaged to continue on across the Atlantic.

The *NC-4* successfully completed the 1,381-mile leg from Newfoundland to the Azores, landing off the Port of Horta on May 17, fifteen hours and eighteen minutes out of Trepassey Bay. On May 20, it made the 190-mile hop from Horta to Ponta Delgada and on May 27 covered the remaining 800 miles to Lisbon in nine hours and thirty minutes. That meant victory, because the Atlantic at last had been crossed by air.

But the scheduled final destination was Plymouth and after a three-day pause in Lisbon, the *NC-4* set out for England. Another stop had to be made at Figuerra, in Portugal, to carry out some minor adjustments on the flying boat and by the time these were completed it was too late to reach Plymouth before nightfall. So the *NC-4* was able to continue its journey that day only as far as Ferrol, in Spain, which was a rather odd coincidence. It was at this very spot that Columbus supposedly fitted out his three small ships before embarking on his own great and audacious trans-Atlantic adventure more than five centuries earlier.

The *NC-4* continued on to Plymouth, where it arrived at 1:30 P.M. on May 31, to the wild acclaim of huge throngs gathered along the waterfront.

It had taken fifteen days to complete that first Atlantic crossing, but the *NC-4,* which now stands on display at the American National Air Museum in Washington, had become firmly enshrined in world aviation history.

There still remained to be won, in the contest between the mighty Atlantic and the flimsy flying machines of man, a prize which would gain for the winner not only a great deal of international glory, but also the respectable reward of £10,000 in cash. Just before the First World War, British press baron Lord Northcliffe's London *Daily Mail,* which had previously offered and paid cash prizes for the first flight across the English Channel, the first flight from London to Manchester and the first circuit of Britain, extended its interest to much wider horizons by offering this handsome sum for the first nonstop flight across the Atlantic.

Early in 1919, several aircraft and their crews began to gather in Newfoundland to prepare for a crack at the *Daily Mail's* prize. The aircraft were shipped out from Britain by sea and assembled and tested upon their arrival in Newfoundland. One of these machines was a specially built Sopwith biplane powered by a single Rolls-Royce Eagle engine and named the *Atlantic.* Its crew consisted of pilot Harry Hawker and his navigator, Lieutenant-Commander Kenneth Mackenzie-Grieve, R.N.

The *Atlantic* was already poised near Placentia Bay for its attempt to cross the ocean when news arrived that the *NC-4* had managed to reach Plymouth. Two days later, in spite of unfavorable weather reports, the *Atlantic* took off in a twenty-mile-an-hour crosswind from what must have been a horrifyingly short and bumpy airstrip—only about 600 yards long—and managed to stagger into the sky with its heavy fuel load. Once it was airborne and over the sea, the *Atlantic*'s undercarriage was jettisoned to reduce weight and drag, and the machine slowly climbed to its cruising altitude of 10,000 feet. It maintained a comfortable speed of 105 miles-an-hour until 10:00 P.M., when it was tossed and mauled by violent gales and hammered by torrential rains.

As some cautious and suspicious pilot once said, when one thing goes wrong quite often almost everything else goes wrong. Certainly, in the case of the *Atlantic* the encounter with extremely bad weather was followed almost immediately by some ominous readings on the thermometer which monitored the engine heat. Hawker opened the shutters in front of the radiator, but the engine temperature continued to climb. For several hours the pilot nursed the Sopwith along as best he could. But by the break of dawn, it had become obvious that the ailing engine could not continue to function much longer. Hawker prepared to make a descent into the sea after his navigator had ascertained that they were not far south of one of the regular shipping lanes. Their hope was to stay aloft until they spotted a ship that could come to their rescue. But even this rather forlorn possibility seemed to vanish for a few hair-raising minutes. Having switched off his engine in an attempt to cool it by gliding powerless from 6,000 feet, Hawker found that it would not start when he restored ignition. Grieve furiously operated the hand-pump to force more fuel into the carburetors. Scarcely more than ten feet above the menacing rollers on the wind-tossed waters of the Atlantic, the engine of the aircraft suddenly responded with a welcome roar and the airmen were able to climb skyward once more.

At last they caught a glimpse of a vessel through the misty haze and went down to circle it twice, firing off red flares from their Very pistol to signal their distress. They made a remarkably smooth landing considering the condition of the seas, near the Danish vessel, *Mary*. Part of the rear upper fuselage of the *Atlantic* was designed so that it could be removed and used as a boat in just such an emergency, and the two flyers lost no time in detaching and boarding it while their helpless aircraft wallowed in the ocean. After a great deal of effort in the raging seas, a boat from the *Mary* managed to pick them up and carry them to safety. Thus ended the first attempt at a nonstop aerial crossing of the Atlantic.

Strange as it might seem in these modern days of worldwide instant communication, many days passed before those who were anxiously awaiting news of the fate of the *Atlantic* learned that its crew and much of the aircraft itself had been plucked out of the ocean. The *Mary* had no wireless equipment and when days went by without word of the aircraft and its crew, the fliers were given up for dead. While the ship that had rescued the airmen was still plodding its way toward Great Britain, King Georve V sent messages of condolence to their families. The Royal letter to Mrs. Hawker read: "The King, fearing the worst must now be realised regarding the fate of your husband, wishes to express his deep sympathy and that of the Queen in your sudden and tragic sorrow. His Majesty feels that the nation has lost one of its most able and daring pilots, who sacrificed his life for the fame and honour of British flying."

It was not until the *Mary* was off the Butt of Lewis, Scotland, that flag signals sent to the shore informed the world that Hawker and Grieves had survived their ordeal. But there would be many, in the years which followed, who would take off along this treacherous glory road from Newfoundland and never be seen again.

On June 14, 1919, two young Englishmen, John Alcock and Arthur Whitten Brown, made their final inspection of the Vickers Vimy twin-engined biplane in which they hoped to cross the ocean. The aircraft sat ready for takeoff at a makeshift airstrip from which some of the rocks and humps had been removed, in a place called Lester's Field, near Monday's Pool, Newfoundland.

Shortly past four o'clock that afternoon, after waiting for the wind to die down, and completing the repair of some minor damage to a fuel line, Alcock and Brown climbed into the open cockpit of the Vickers Vimy and after warming up the Rolls-Royce engines, raced down the bumpy field in a slightly crosswind direction. For some distance after takeoff the aircraft's landing gear was barely grazing the tree tops. Heavily loaded to about eleven pounds per square foot of lifting surface, the biplane climbed slowly but steadily into the eastern sky.

At 5:20 P.M., while flying at 1,500 feet and still slowly climbing, the airmen observed ahead of them haze that was rapidly growing heavier and thicker. Brown decided to tap out a message on his wireless telegraph. While he was in the act of doing so, a blade of the small propeller which operated the wind-driven generator suddenly broke off. That was the end of any transmissions to the world below for the rest of the flight. The increasing cloud cover prevented Brown from using his sextant. When they climbed out of this layer, they found themselves situated between it and another one about 5,000 feet up. Navigation had to be done by dead reckoning, made more difficult by the unexpectedly strong tailwinds. Shortly after midnight, Brown was able to spot the star Vega and the trusty Pole Star through a brief opening in the clouds. From subsequent observations with his sextant, he was able to determine that they had covered about 650 nautical miles since leaving Newfoundland, at an average ground speed of 106 knots.

Throughout the night they made steady and fairly uneventful progress across the ocean. Then, just after encountering the early dawn which seems to race so swiftly toward an eastbound aircraft, the Vickers Vimy suddenly entered an area of dense cloud from which it appeared impossible to find an exit. Even the aircraft's wingtips and the forward part of its fuselage became lost to view. The men were flying blind, a potentially deadly condition indeed in those early days of aviation before the advent of today's sophisticated instruments.

As often happens in such a situation when all horizons disappear and there are no substitutes provided by the proper instruments, the airmen eventually lost their sense of balance and direction. The aircraft began to perform peculiar gyrations as though it had suddenly developed a will of its own and the revolving compass needle told them they were falling in either a spin or a very deep spiral. The altimeter readings rapidly dropped from 3,000 to 2,000 feet and finally to a mere 500 feet, while the airplane was still surrounded by the impenetrable mists. When they plunged abruptly into clear air, they were not more than 100 feet above the surface of the sea. The water appeared to be not below them but standing up beside them, due to the wide angle at which the airplane was tilted against the horizontal when they emerged from the cloud. Throwing on full throttle and centralizing the airplane's control stick and rudder bar, Alcock managed at the last moment to bring the machine into proper flying position.

Next, they ran into heavy rain, then snow mingled with sleet, and finally, hail. After climbing to 8,800 feet without being able to get above the foul weather, the airmen discovered that the face of a vital fuel gauge, fixed in an exposed position on the center-section struts, had become clogged with snow and was no longer readable. Up there amid the hail, sleet and snow, more than 8,000 feet above the Atlantic, Brown had to crawl out of the cockpit and clear the face of the gauge with one hand and maintain his balance on the slippery surface of the fuselage by holding on to a strut with the other hand. The control surfaces of the aircraft picked up some ice for awhile but it finally melted away when the machine was taken down to a lower altitude.

At 8:15 on the morning of June 15, Arthur Whitten Brown had just finished a cup of coffee from a vacuum bottle and had turned to replace it in a compartment behind the cockpit when John Alcock grabbed his shoulder excitedly and pulled him around. Although Brown could not hear the words of his companion over the roar of the engines, he could see his lips moving as he pointed downward and ahead. With his gaze following the outstretched finger, Brown saw two tiny specks of land which turned out to be the small islands of Eeshal and Turbot, lying off the coast of Ireland. Crossing the coast at 8:25 A.M., the flyers soon spotted the tall masts of the wireless station at Clifden. The Vickers Vimy still had ample fuel to complete the journey through to London, but heavy clouds and mists were lying low enough to obscure the hilltops. Alcock decided to land, instead of trying to fly on to London through such dangerously unfavorable weather. A smooth-looking field appeared not far from the wireless station. After carefully looking it over, Alcock glided down to a landing. But the nice level expanse of green turned out to be a peat bog, and the wheels of the big biplane sank into it deeply. The machine finally ended up with its nose sunk into the muck. Although the aircraft was quite severely damaged, its pilot and navigator clambered out unharmed, fifteen hours and fifty-seven minutes after taking off from Newfoundland. When a ceremony was held a short time later in London to present the *Daily Mail's* prize to the first men to fly nonstop across the Atlantic Ocean, the check was handed to them by a most enthusiastic aviation buff named Winston Churchill, Secretary of State for War. He announced with much satisfaction that the King had seen fit to bestow upon the latest national heroes the titles of Knight Commanders of the Order of the British Empire.

On December 18 of that same year, Sir John Alcock was killed, at the age of twenty-seven, when his Vickers Vimy aircraft, enroute from Brooklands to Paris, crashed in heavy fog in northern France. Deeply affected by this sudden tragedy, Sir Arthur Whitten Brown never flew again.

Although there were a few sporadic and unsuccessful attempts to fly the Atlantic not long after Alcock and Brown's accomplishment, it would be another eight years before their record was broken by a shy and gangling young man from Missouri named Charles Augustus Lindbergh.

He has since been called, and with good reason, "the last hero." There seems little doubt that his feat in flying solo from New York to Paris in thirty-three hours and thirty minutes was the greatest single-handed exploit in the history of aviation. The fabled "Lone Eagle" certainly had all the attributes of a genuine American folk hero—shy, modest, previously unknown to the general public. Above all, he possessed an almost fantastic degree of stubborn courage which carried him over insurmountable odds to something as close to undying glory as most mortals ever achieve.

His flight began at 7:52 A.M. on May 20, 1927, from Roosevelt Field, Long Island, in a little Ryan monoplane called the *Spirit of St. Louis*. Those of the modern generation, accustomed to the aerial leviathans which now wing across the Atlantic, shake their heads in wonder when they see the flimsy-looking little machine hanging, almost toy-like, from the ceiling of the Aeronautical Museum of the Smithsonian Institution in Washington, D.C. Yet that seemingly puny contraption, scarcely larger than one of today's small sports planes, kept humming away in awful solitude, without cough or splutter, for 3,610 miles from New York to Paris. It arrived there almost two hours ahead of its original schedule, with enough fuel left in its tanks to continue another 700 miles right on to Rome if its weary pilot had so desired.

The machine performed, to use Lindbergh's words, "like a living creature, gliding along smoothly, happily, as though a successful flight means as much to it as to me . . . . *We* have made this flight across the ocean, not *I* or *it*."

When he set out upon his legendary flight, this young man was not some callow and inexperienced youth depending upon sheer luck to get him to Paris. He was a former military and airmail pilot with several thousands of air hours in his log book and it would be safe to say that no attempt to fly the Atlantic was ever preceded by more careful study and preparation than that of the *Spirit of St. Louis*. Lindbergh sacrificed every possible item aboard the aircraft in the interest of greater fuel capacity. Even the cockpit windshield was dispensed with, in order to make room for an extra fuel tank forward of the pilot. The only way he could see directly out of his aircraft was through the side windows, although a small periscope device had been installed to allow at least an occasional peep ahead. He decided to make the flight without radio equipment, in order to save weight. He didn't even take along a spare suit and had to remain in his flying garb after reaching Paris until some other clothing could be purchased for him.

With no radio, the Lone Eagle was truly and completely alone. After covering the 1,000-mile leg from Long Island to Newfoundland, he had to circle low over St. John's, before heading eastward across the sea. This he did in the hope that observers there would relay to his friends and backers and the rest of the world that he had completed that stage of the long journey safely. (By then he had been flying for eleven hours.)

On the way across the Atlantic he had to make frequent course changes to avoid icing conditions and other forms of unfavorable weather. At the end of twenty-four hours of flying through a deserted and forbidding world of water and sky, he at last spotted a few small fishing boats below him. By that time he was becoming a little concerned about the accuracy of his navigation, after so many course shifts. He flew down to circle over the craft, yelling out of the monoplane's side window, "Which way is Ireland?" But the fishermen could only gawk in speechless wonder.

Lindbergh landed at Le Bourget airfield at 10:22 P.M., Paris time, on May 21. His progress during the final stages of the flight had been observed from below and by the time he landed in Paris the airport was swarming with an estimated 100,000 wildly excited French welcomers. A legend had been born. America's conquering hero, after flying a few days later to

England, was triumphantly carried home, along with his marvelous little aircraft, aboard the cruiser *Memphis,* flagship of the U. S. European Fleet, at the order of President Calvin Coolidge. The traditional ticker tape parade up Broadway was the greatest that avenue for homecoming heroes had ever witnessed.

In the years immediately following Lindbergh's great achievement, there were numerous successful and, more often, unsuccessful attempts to fly the Atlantic, in which a great many of the brave or foolhardy lost their lives. Some of them took place with considerable backing, preparation and publicity. At least one, that of Douglas "Wrong Way" Corrigan, occurred with scarcely anyone knowing what he was up to until he had arrived safely in Dublin. The young Irishman later blithely explained that after the U.S. aviation authorities had forebade him to try an ocean crossing because of the doubtful condition of his aircraft, he had taken off to fly southwest from New York. Confused by his compass, he had somehow flown in an entirely different direction to that which he so sincerely had in mind.

The story of trans-Atlantic flight began with a series of bold and hair-raising gambles and experiments tried, quite often, in quest of adventure, fame and fortune, rather than in any profound search for scientific and technical knowledge. In some cases, the chances of survival were roughly equivalent to those encountered in going over Niagara Falls in a barrel. Yet, more and more knowledge *was* acquired, which eventually led to the first cautious attempts in 1939, by Pan-American Airways and Imperial Airways, to establish with their *Clipper* and *Empire* flying boats fairly regular *summer* passenger-carrying schedules across the Atlantic by way of the Azores.

This, then, was in general terms the position of trans-Atlantic aviation up to the time when many of the events described in this story began to take place.

It remained for the awesome urgency of another world war and the sheer weight of concentrated manpower and technological effort to strip from trans-

Atlantic flight some of its mystery and menace, if not all of its problems. The wartime Atlantic aerial ferry operation, in its evolving forms and titles—from Canadian Pacific Air Services to the British Ministry of Aircraft Production's "Atfero," to Royal Air Force Ferry and then Transport Command—safely delivered to the war front more than 10,000 airplanes of various types and sizes. Its astonishing success undoubtedly created the solid foundation for today's vast network of trans-Atlantic air routes which now span that great ocean. The achievement of regular and reliable overseas air traffic was hastened by many years as a result of what these Ferry Command pilots learned in so many hard and dangerous ways.

This year an average of approximately 27,500 passengers will embark each day upon the 230 regular trans-Atlantic flights operated by twenty-one different airlines. The trip that took Charles Lindbergh thirty-three hours and thirty minutes from New York to Paris is now carried out in huge and luxurious sky ships in about seven-and-a-half hours. This time soon may be cut to three-and-a-half hours, by such aircraft as the supersonic Concorde.

But a little more than three decades ago, men such as those who appear in the following pages faced the perils of trans-Atlantic flight again and again, for month after month, in winter and in summer, until at last the old nightmare lost a great deal of its dark terror and became instead the final and quite glorious realization of a long-cherished dream.

Among the particularly distinguished aircrews of R.A.F. Ferry Command who took part in this saga was that of a famed Consolidated B-24 Liberator bomber called the *Commando* which, under the command of Captain William J. Vanderkloot, a twenty-six-year-old American civilian pilot, safely carried across many thousands of danger-filled miles more wartime leaders than any other Allied aircraft.

Chapter One

O n an afternoon late in July of 1942, Captain Bill
Vanderkloot was sitting in his room in London's
Savoy Hotel contemplating his sedate surroundings.
He wondered what new excitement and pleasures the
ancient city might have to offer him and his crew during their latest visit to a metropolis that could still
provide some interesting night life, even in wartime,
behind the blackout curtains of its countless pubs and
cafes.

Snugly bedded down at an airfield not far from
the city was a huge, black, four-engined Liberator
bomber that Vanderkloot and his crew had just flown
across the North Atlantic from Dorval, near Montreal,
by way of Prestwick, near Glasgow. The big bomber,
which had been converted into a passenger-carrying
machine for "V.I.P."'s engaged in various urgent wartime missions, was called the *Commando,* in honor of
Admiral Lord Louis Mountbatten, head of the British
Combined Operations or "Commando" forces. During
a trans-Atlantic flight, he had been one of the first of a
long list of personages to be carried by the aircraft during the course of the war.

Before setting out to partake of what the city had
to offer, *Commando*'s crew planned to have dinner
together. They made a closely knit group, both in the
air and on the ground. Co-pilot Jack Ruggles was
another American, who hailed from San Francisco.
Radio operator Russ Holmes, who could get an amaz-

ing amount out of the comparatively crude electronic equipment then carried aboard such aircraft, came from Toronto. Flight Engineer John Affleck called London, Ontario, his home town and his partner, Flight Engineer Ron Williams, was from Centreville, Nova Scotia. The fact that two engineers had been assigned to the job of preserving the good health of the big bird was an indication of the importance the R.A.F. Ferry Command attached to *Commando's* journeys into far-off and sometimes out-of-the-way places of the world, where adequate maintenance for such a large aircraft might not be readily available at all times.

Captain Vanderkloot had just carefully extracted a clean shirt from his small travelling bag when he was interrupted by a typically polite and gentle English tinkle of his telephone. The call turned out to be from the Air Ministry, no less, requesting that he present himself at an office in King Charles Street as soon as possible.

Going downstairs, he crossed the Savoy's stately lobby with peculiar misgivings and questions running through his mind, wondering why in the world he, Bill Vanderkloot, was being summoned so abruptly to the Air Ministry. He couldn't recall having done anything bad enough to get him hauled up on the carpet, but it was hard to tell. He might accidentally have committed some grave sin he didn't even know about. He was still occupied with such vaguely disturbing thoughts when the doorman whistled up a cab for him.

Bill was about to give him a half crown for his trouble but then, after hesitating a moment, decided to present him with four bob. After all, handing the doorman at the Savoy a half crown was almost like handing a major-general a half crown. Bill Vanderkloot, on his way to see the brass at the Air Ministry about the Lord knew what, didn't want to have his morale further impaired by a cold and disapproving stare from the magnificently uniformed guardian of the Savoy's front door.

His mild puzzlement collapsed into complete and utter bewilderment when he arrived at the Air Ministry and learned who had ordered him to be there and was at that moment awaiting his arrival in an inner office. It was not merely an Air Commodore or even an Air Vice Marshal. It was none other, in fact, than Air Chief Marshal Sir Charles Portal, head of the Royal Air Force. As he waited tensely in the anteroom outside Portal's office, Bill concluded nervously that if he were about to be bawled out or fired about something, at least he would be departing from Ferry Command on a first class basis. He couldn't recall any Ferry Command captain ever having been fired personally by the Chief of the R.A.F.

When finally he was ushered through the doorway into Sir Charles's office, he found himself facing a lean, dark man with a rather large and sharp nose set between keen, bright eyes like those of an eagle. Waving him to a seat before his desk, Portal sat back for a few moments and surveyed Bill closely. Then he smiled in a friendly enough fashion and opened the conversation with some casual questions about how Vanderkloot was enjoying the sights of London and how things had gone on his recently completed flight to Bathurst in West Africa with Lord Swinton.

After a few moments of small talk, Sir Charles placed the tips of his long, slim fingers together and gazed at Bill Vanderkloot intently. Finally he spoke:

"We have another V.I.P. assignment for you," he said. "It involves a person we would rather not subject to the injections which might be required if he had to make intermediate stops in Africa on his way to Cairo. Come over here."

Portal stood up and walked across the room to a large map on the wall.

"If you were setting out to fly from London to Cairo in the most direct way possible, how would you go about it?" he asked.

Bill Vanderkloot studied the map for awhile and then began to trace a route with his finger.

"Setting out from here," he said, "I would fly directly to Gibraltar, in one hop. On the next evening, I would proceed eastward along the Mediterranean until last light, before cutting across Tunisia and on to Cairo, with the hope of reaching the Nile shortly after dawn. In that way, we'd have the protection of the night against any enemy aircraft we might possibly meet along the way. It would involve two very long hops, but with the Liberator's range, I don't think that would present too much of a problem."

They discussed at some length *Commando*'s previous performances in trans-Atlantic hops and her recent long circuit from London to Gibraltar to West Africa to Egypt and back to England. Portal questioned Vanderkloot on every detail of this lengthy journey.

Vanderkloot assured Portal that he had great confidence in the skill and ingenuity of flight engineers Affleck and Williams, who were familiar with every last bolt, nut, and rivet in the big bomber. With the combined talents of two such topnotch mechanics available to *Commando,* Vanderkloot felt there was little to fear about maintaining the machine in first class working order no matter where its errands might take it.

"Very well," said Portal, at the close of their conversation. "Thank you for your opinions, and stay handy to a telephone for the next while."

They shook hands at the door—civilian pilots of Ferry Command didn't do much saluting in those days—and Bill Vanderkloot returned to the Savoy, still puzzled but quite elated. No dressing down. An extremely friendly reception, in fact, by the legendary man in whose lean and capable hands lay the tremendous responsibility of directing Britain's air war against the Axis powers.

It was a happy coincidence, which fitted perfectly his relieved frame of mind, when Bill encountered in the bar at the Savoy several uniformed officers of the U.S. Army who had just arrived in London. Somehow, war correspondent Quentin Reynolds became mixed up in the jolly dinner party that followed and lasted into the night. Next morning, while trying to sort out the various incidents of the hectic preceding evening, at least two facts lingered quite vividly in Bill Vanderkloot's mind. One was that after the big reunion dinner with his countrymen, marked by a huge number of horribly expensive toasts, only Bill and his co-pilot, Jack Ruggles, were finally left at the table to pick up the astronomical tab. This he and Ruggles had signed with trembling hand, while darkly wondering how in hell they would ever manage to find enough money to bail themselves out of the posh place when it was time to leave.

The other sharply etched and haunting recollection was that during a very late visit to the suite of Quentin Reynolds, he had discovered, in a trip to the bathroom, that the famous writer kept several frisky goldfish in the bidet.

It was fairly late on the second evening after his meeting with Portal that Bill Vanderkloot received another call from the Air Ministry. It was to advise him that he would be picked up shortly by an R.A.F. staff car, which would be awaiting him at the doorway of the Savoy. He was given no other information. It didn't greatly relieve his mystification when, upon climbing into the car at the appointed hour, he found the driver to be quite vague about their destination as they headed through the streets of London in the blackout. Even in daylight, Bill was not yet sufficiently familiar with the myriad byways of the great city to know his way around for much more than a block or two from the Strand Palace or the Savoy. Now, in the darkness, he was completely confused, which might sound curious for a man who could safely find his way across vast oceans and deserts in an airplane. Actually, it was a phenomenon much more common than might be expected among earthbound pilots forced to navigate London's twisting thoroughfares by street signs instead of by the more familiar stars.

At last the car came to a halt at the head of a small and rather narrow street.

"I have been told to instruct you, sir," said the driver, "to walk down this street until you reach a door on your right, where you will see a very dim light. You are to knock upon that door and identify yourself when it is opened to you. You are being expected. Goodnight sir."

Now completely baffled by the circumstances surrounding his presence there, Bill walked down the darkened street. And to this day he is still baffled, because somehow no one ever took the trouble to explain to him just why it was necessary to cover on foot those last few yards of that short and fateful journey.

Arriving at the designated door, he knocked and it was opened by a household servant.

"My name is Captain Vanderkloot," he announced.

"Ah, yes sir," said the servant. "Come right this way."

He was then ushered into a study at 10 Downing Street where, clad in a blue dressing gown and smoking one of the biggest cigars Bill Vanderkloot had ever seen, sat Prime Minister Winston Churchill.

"Sit down, Captain Vanderkloot," said he, his pink and rather cherubic features breaking into an almost mischievous smile. "I understand we're going to Cairo! Do you care for a drink?"

The dumbfounded Vanderkloot decided that at this particular moment a scotch and soda might be a very good idea, indeed.

They chatted for some time about the proposed trip, before Churchill arose from his chair. Forever afterward, Bill Vanderkloot was to remember the utter fascination with which, at that important moment in his life, he studied Mr. Churchill's carpet slippers. They were blue and had the letters "P.M." embroidered in gold on the toes!

"When would you prefer to leave for Cairo?" the prime minister asked.

"Well, sir, if I had a choice," said Vanderkloot, "I'd like to leave as closely as possible to midnight and in as bad weather as it is practical to fly in. A midnight takeoff should bring us into Gibraltar at about the right time, with most of the flight under cover of darkness. Bad weather here over the British Isles might cut down our chances of running into enemy aircraft during this critical stage of the flight."

"Very well," said Churchill. "I'll give you a margin of four days in which to pick your night!"

So ended the first meeting of the prime minister and the young pilot who was to fly him for many thousands of hazardous miles.

Churchill's determination to make a personal inspection of the situation in the Middle East, no matter what risks might be involved in such a long and audacious aerial journey, was based on an increasing anxiety concerning the discouraging events which had taken place in that area. The desert army of General Erwin Rommel had subjected the British forces under General Claude Auchinleck to one disastrous defeat after another. Tobruk had already fallen and Rommel's highly mechanized, fast moving army had pursued the British forces farther and farther into Egypt, until the Eighth Army was now preparing a desperate last stand at El Alemein, almost on the very threshold of Cairo itself.

In his book *The Hinge of Fate*, the prime minister later described some of the events leading up to the curious meeting which had taken place between him and the bewildered young American pilot that night at 10 Downing Street:

The doubts I had about the High Command in the Middle East were fed continually by the reports which I received from many quarters. It became urgently necessary for me to go there and settle the decisive questions on the spot. It was at first accepted that this journey would be by Gibraltar and Takoradi and thence across Central Africa to Cairo, involving five or even six days' flying. As this would carry me through tropical and malarious regions, a whole series of protective injections was prescribed. Some of these would take ten days to give their immunity, and involved considerable discomfort and even inactivity meanwhile. Several members of the War Cabinet also took a very close and friendly interest in my health and became an opposing factor to be reasoned with.

However, at this juncture there arrived in England a

young American pilot, Captain Vanderkloot, who had just flown from the United States (*sic*) in the aeroplane 'Commando', a Liberator plane from which the bomb-racks had been removed and some sort of passenger accommodation substituted. This machine was certainly capable of flying along the route prescribed with good margins in hand at all stages. Portal, the Chief of the Air Staff, saw this pilot and cross-examined him about 'Commando'. Vanderkloot, who had already flown a million miles, asked why it was necessary to fly all around Takoradi, Kano, Fort Lamy, El Obeid, etc. He said he could make one bound from Gibraltar to Cairo, flying from Gibraltar eastward in the afternoon, turning sharply across Spanish or Vichy territory as dusk fell, and then proceeding eastward till he struck the Nile about Assiout, when a turn to the northward would bring us in another hour or so to the Cairo landing-ground northwest of the Pyramids. This altered the whole picture, I could be in Cairo in two days without any trouble about Central African bugs and the inoculations against them. Portal was convinced.

That night when he went to bed in his room at the Savoy after his first meeting with his distinguished prospective passenger—and, indeed, his first inkling of whom it was to be—Bill Vanderkloot lay there projecting in his mind what might have been called a special, wide-screen, technicolor production of a series of mental pictures which usually preceded an important mission. It was his habit to "pre-fly" such trips in as much detail as his imagination could muster. Compass headings, altitudes, estimated times to cover various legs of the route, alternate landings points—if they were available—in case of aircraft malfunctions, weather problems or other emergencies . . . all such factors he usually carefully considered as far in advance as possible, as a routine prelude to a long flight. In the case of this particular mission, he lay there wide awake far into the night, considering over and over again every contingency that might be encountered along the thousands of miles of highly dangerous skies which lay between London and Cairo.

When he was called to the Air Ministry next day

for another conference with Air Chief Marshal Portal, he learned a little more about what he could expect in the way of protection and assistance from the R.A.F.

"You will have no fighter escort across the south of England to the sea," said Portal. "Any such precaution might do more to draw enemy attention or action than avoid it. Instead, all R.A.F. aircraft in the area will remain grounded until you have reached the open sea.

"But we have arranged a system of signal lights which will be flashed from the ground—visibility permitting—as you pass over any of our stations along the way. Green will signify that all is clear. Yellow will indicate that there is a possibility of enemy air activity in your vicinity. And red will mean close danger.

"One other thing. I am not to be told any details of the exact route of your flight plan. It goes without saying, of course, that neither is any other person to know such details, except yourself and your crew, who may be informed after you are airborne. We know your departure points and destinations. Details of anything that lies in between these two facts must remain secret, even to me. Certainly, to that extent, you are on your own . . . . Good luck."

With that, Bill Vanderkloot was sent upon his way by the lean and shrewd-eyed man who personally had selected him for this historic mission and who, in time, would be included himself in the impressive roster of those flown by the young pilot of *Commando* as, eventually, she carried almost every top-ranking member of the British High Command.

Sir Charles Wilson (later Lord Moran), who was Churchill's personal physician, described in his diary the prime minister's jubilant announcement to his colleagues that he'd found a better and swifter way to make the long journey from London to Cairo:

I was summoned this morning to No. 10 Downing Street, where I heard that we should soon be on the move. The P.M. has decided to fly to Cairo. From Gibraltar he will fly south to Takoradi on the Gold Coast, and so across Central Africa to Cairo. It means five days in the air, landing at places where malaria and yellow fever are rife. The

P.M. wanted my advice about inoculations. I did not like the plan and gave my reasons.

As I was leaving I met John Anderson (Lord President of the Council). He said that certain members of the Cabinet were concerned about the Prime Minister's travels and the dangers he was running in flying over hostile territory in an unarmed bomber . . . .

At the appointed hour I joined them in the Cabinet Room. I was most concerned with the actual risk of the protective measures against yellow fever. While we were discussing these problems, the door opened and the Prime Minister hurried in, beaming at us disarmingly— always a sign that he was up to mischief. He began to unfold a large map, spreading it on the table.

"Vanderkloot says it is quite unnecessary to fly so far south. He has explained to me that we can fly in one hop to Cairo. Come here and look."

Sir John knelt on a chair to get nearer the map, while (Sir Stafford) Cripps leant over his shoulder. The P.M. with a pencil, traced the route from Gibraltar across Spanish Morocco till he struck the Nile, where his pencil turned sharply to the north.

"This changes the whole picture," the P.M. added confidently.

I ventured to ask who Vanderkloot was. It appeared that he had just crossed the Atlantic in a bomber, and it is in this machine that we are to fly to Cairo. I wondered why it was left to an American pilot to find a safe way to Cairo, but that did not seem a profitable line of speculation.

"You see, Charles, we need not bother about inoculations."

Anderson and Cripps pored over the map like excited schoolboys, and the party broke up without a word of warning or remonstrance about the risks of the P.M. flying over hostile territory in an unarmed bomber by daylight. The P.M. gets his own way with everyone with hardly a murmur.

Although the risks of the prime minister's proposed journey would indeed be considerable, they were perhaps being exaggerated to a small degree by Sir Charles in at least two respects. *Commando* was armed to the extent of carrying two 50 m.m. cannons, one fitted in the tail and the other in the nose. And

most of her long journey to Cairo would be under-
taken not by daylight but by night, under conditions
Vanderkloot greatly preferred in carrying out such
critical missions. Darkness provided an extra margin
of safety for the big black converted bomber. The
night hours also permitted, when the skies were sufficiently clear, the higher degree of accuracy in cor-
recting *Commando*'s course, accuracy that could be
attained only by the precise star shots required in celestial navigation.

Chapter Two

Bill Vanderkloot's love affair with airplanes had begun very early and was to last for a long, long time.

Although it probably could have been called a pure and simple case of love at first sight, it began as a one-sided courtship, carried on shyly and from afar. On a clear day in Lake Bluff, Illinois, where Bill spent his childhood, he could look out three miles across the waters of Lake Michigan toward the Great Lakes Naval Air Station and see the lumbering flying boats taking off and landing. Jaunty plumes of spray were tossed aloft by their sleek hulls and the sun glinted brightly from their wide and shining wings.

To the eyes of a twelve-year-old, these huge and distant birds, soaring and dipping with the ease of seagulls yet setting the sky to thundering with the powerful throb of their engines, seemed like steeds of the gods.

And it still was an age, back in 1929, when pilots did appear to be rather godlike men, garbed in their great leather flying suits and helmets and scarves not only worn for dash and warmth but also used as handy wiping cloths to rub the oil splatters off their goggles. (An aircraft engine in those days that didn't throw at least some oil from its busy rocker-boxes back into the face of its pilot was so rare as to be virtually unknown.)

Not that Bill Vanderkloot ever had much opportunity, at that stage of his fascination with airplanes, to even lay eyes upon any pilots at close range. He had never had the chance of actually visiting the Great Lakes Training Station to stand nearby as the big flying boats came and went on their mysterious errands. Their arrivals and departures were always distant things, over on the horizon across the waters, but they became so familiar that for Bill they grew to be a part of his daily wide panorama of sky and water and clouds.

The population of Lake Bluff was than about 850. It was a quiet little community, thirty-five miles north of Chicago where Bill's father commuted to his steel fabrication business. The principal edifices of commerce along Main Street consisted of a general store, a small grocery store and a dry cleaning establishment. There was also a library, a post office and a police department made up of the chief and one constable. The agent at the little railway station was also the baggageman, ticket seller and telegraph operator.

When he was fourteen, Bill left Lake Bluff to attend Culver Military Academy, an experience he was to enjoy greatly during the next four years. He became captain of the boxing team (for a while he entertained the idea of becoming a professional) and eventually became the leader of the academy's famed Black Horse Cavalry Troop, an impressive unit of 125 jet-black mounts which still represents Culver at such important events as the Washington parade during a presidential inauguration. It was a particularly proud day for Cadet Bill Vanderkloot when he led his troop through the streets of Chicago at the opening ceremonies of the World Fair in 1933.

Although he was greatly taken up with the life at Culver, one of his most exciting discoveries while attending the military academy had nothing to do with the school curriculum. It was made during summer vacation time and marked what was one of the most important turning points of his life. He found Sky Harbour.

Sky Harbour, not far from the Lake Bluff, was a small airfield where itinerant barnstormers operated their wood-wire-and-fabric aircraft. They provided five-dollars-a-flip sightseeing flights and flying lessons for those who had the money and the desire. Bill didn't have much money but he had a lot of desire, something he fully realized for the first time as he stood one afternoon at Sky Harbour in the slipstream blast of a Waco biplane revving up for takeoff.

Airplanes didn't stink then, the way the big jet jobs do today. The slipstream of an airplane warming up its engine in a hay field bore to the nostrils a most intriguing blend of scents; far more captivating to an airstruck youngster than the perfume of any glamorous *femme galante* to the nose of a Stagedoor Johnny.

It was a wild, free smell, bearing a mixture of the strangely sweet odor of hot oil, shellac and cedar, swept on a gale that hammered the face and flattened the grass and sang a song of tremendous power, of straining to be off and away into the sky. It was the very smell of flight itself, now largely gone from the enclosed and elaborately instrumented cockpits of most modern aircraft. But in the days of open cockpit planes it was always there, fresher and clearer the higher you climbed into the thin, crisp air upon which float the clouds called stratocumulus.

Like some young pilgrim on his way to regular worship, Bill Vanderkloot began to make the trek to Sky Harbour at every opportunity, there to watch the airplanes waddle like clumsy ducks across the rutted field. Then, having barely attained a speed which thickened the flimsy and treacherous air beneath their outstretched wings, they climbed steadily skyward with wondrous grace and beauty.

So constantly did Bill Vanderkloot haunt Sky Harbour that the pilots came to know him as "that airstruck kid" who was always hiking over from Lake Bluff. His father gave him enough spending money to allow an occasional airplane ride, but it wasn't long until he was earning the odd brief flight on his own, by doing chores for the barnstormers.

It was a time when airplanes needed all the ground they could get for a successful takeoff. A strong and willing lad was a handy fellow to have about when you had to turn an airplane around at the very edge of the farthest fence. Bill rode downwind on the stepsection of the wing beside the fuselage until the airplane ran out of field. He then hopped off and pressed his shoulder heavily against one wingtip while the pilot furiously gunned the motor to achieve as short a turnabout as possible, in order to conserve every precious foot of sod for the takeoff.

When the airplane finally bellowed off with a jaunty farewell flip of its rudder, Bill had to tramp the long route back to the upwind end of the field to await his next aeronautical assignment. On a busy weekend, including the return hikes between Lake Bluff and Sky Harbour, he travelled many miles on foot.

These and other chores for a keen lad all led to a few extra minutes of air time, some of it even at one of the sticks of a dual-control aircraft! Pilots being the kind of men they were in those days couldn't resist the appealing enthusiasm of a kid who so desperately wanted to fly. It was almost a religious phenomenon, in which the true believer, no matter how young and tender he might be, was considered a convert to a kind of holy order. Maybe it still exists. But in those day, it particularly applied to the fliers, for the simple reason that most of them could still well remember when they were very young and keen and couldn't fly.

There were fares to be collected and "blood chits" to be signed by the passengers, theoretically absolving the pilot from all responsibility in the event of a crackup, and gas to be carried and cockpit covers to be snapped into place at the end of the day and elastic cords to be checked on the undercarriage. In those times, long before the invention of airplane shock absorbers, the planes may not have been *powered* by elastic bands, but they certainly depended on them to keep the axles secured to the undercarriage struts.

By the time he was sixteen years of age, Bill Vanderkloot had acquired six hours of dual instruction— some paid for by funds wheedled from his doubtful parents and some earned the hard way, by making himself handy around Sky Harbour—and he was ready for his solo. His entire training course had been a highly informal hit-and-miss affair, utterly without official blessing from the Federal Aviation Administration.

The great day was bright and clear, with a comfortable headwind rippling across the grass on the field of Sky Harbour. The instructor stepped out of the front cockpit of the Waco biplane, its prop sheening in the sun as it was turned idly by its Curtiss OX-5 engine, and performed the then time honored ceremony which has brought to the heart of many a budding pilot mingled feelings of both pride and horror. He extracted from its socket in the front cockpit the "joystick" as it was called, and bid his student adieu by waving the control column high in the air, like an orchestra conductor jauntily signalling the opening bars of the damndest symphony ever joined by a nervous soloist.

As luck would have it, another airplane containing a student and an instructor was sitting up ahead on the bruised expanse of grass that served as an airstrip. Without the benefit of any controller in any tower (because Sky Harbour had no such thing), this plane with its propeller still turning had priority for takeoff. Lasting only a few minutes but seeming like hours, it was a tense wait in which a rookie pilot on his first faltering venture into the sky understandably might experience some misgivings. The first solo is like a high dive into very cold water—the new pilot doesn't care to hang around the shore dunking his toe and wondering whether he really wants to do it. He just wants to have it over and done with as soon as he can.

But Bill Vanderkloot, at sixteen the veteran of six full hours of dual instruction, was a peculiarly unflappable kid. He had something to do he'd wanted to do for a long time and he wanted to do it right. He was far too preoccupied with the job of doing it right to have any time for foolish qualms about the chances of taking that Waco upstairs and bringing it safely back to Sky Harbour all neat and tidy and in one piece.

When the preceding plane had finally cleared the field, after the instructor had appeared to read somewhat leisurely the complete book of air regulations to his student at least three times, Bill eased open the throttle of the Waco and felt the aircraft roll forward, slowly at first and then with quickening pace like a thoroughbred racehorse reaching its stride. And there *was* a resemblance that later occurred quite often to Culver's top young cavalryman as he made the adjustment from the saddle of a horse to the cockpit of a biplane. An airplane, more like a living thing than any other vehicle yet devised by man, was a high-strung and sensitive mount to be guided with what might be called aggressive respect. Perhaps it was more than mere coincidence that at least two of the most legendary airmen of the First World War, the German Manfred von Richthofen, the renowned "Red Baron"; and the Canadian Colonel William Avery Bishop, top ace of the British Royal Flying Corps, came directly from the cavalry to their respective air forces.

Lightened by the absence of an instructor, the Waco cleared the field and climbed with surprising speed. How strange and glorious it was to be up there alone in the sky! But oh how empty seemed that forward cockpit, with no leather-helmeted father confessor, patient adviser and sometimes caustic tyrant sitting up front ready to show the safe way back to earth!

That first circuit, however, ended in such a neat and satisfactory three-point landing that young Bill Vanderkloot could not resist the impulse to run joyfully that day all the way back to the earthbound serenity of Lake Bluff.

Chapter Three

When Bill Vanderkloot finished Culver in 1933 and entered the University of Virginia at Charlottesville, some parental expectations remained that he might give up his foolishness about flying and settle down to study law. There was still hope at home that he would end up as a good, solid, prosperous corporation lawyer, instead of wasting his life galavanting around in such an obviously unsolid element as the high blue sky.

But it was not to be. Still tingling from his taste of flying at Sky Harbour, Bill found it hard to keep his mind upon more prosaic and earthly things, although at nineteen he was now the proud possessor of a Ford Model A roadster of rather elderly vintage. Unfortunately, even at a breathtaking speed of forty miles an hour *on rough roads,* the Model A would rarely leave the ground, except for comparatively short hops over particularly high bumps.

Although many a young college sport might have been quite happy with such a dashing vehicle, Bill Vanderkloot had his heart set on a more romantic and responsive means of transportation. It wasn't surprising, therefore, when he made a deal with Glenn Messer, who owned a small, homebuilt, unlicensed aircraft called an Air Boss, which he kept in a farmer's field not far from the university.

Glenn offered to swap Bill his airplane for the Model A plus $200 in cash. Bill raised the money somewhere, turned over to Messer the keys of the Ford roadster, and was at last the deliriously proud owner of an airplane of his own, such as it was. The little biplane was powered by an early Pratt & Whitney engine called the J-65.

During every break from lectures and examinations thereafter, the unlicensed pilot stole off to that farmer's field to build up flying time in his unlicensed airplane. It had worked out quite well for about seventy hours of solo time, when something happened which might have ended abruptly Bill Vanderkloot's flying career, but which in the long run, probably advanced it immensely.

One day, shortly after takeoff and at a height of only about 500 feet, his engine suddenly spluttered and died. Having neither the altitude nor the speed to try turning back, he had nowhere else to go but straight ahead into a cypress swamp. He managed to mush the little airplane into the tree tops, cushioning the impact enough to escape serious injury to himself. But the Air Boss was a mess, and being a homebuilt machine for which it was impossible to buy ready-made spare parts, it had to be sold for junk.

When Bill's mother and father heard the news, his mother was elated to know her son had not been hurt. She figured that this would be the blessed end of all the flying nonsense. But his father viewed the matter differently.

"It seems to me the boy is determined he's going to fly," said he. "And if we can't get that damned fool notion out of his head, we may just as well see to it that he does it properly."

And so to Bill Vanderkloot's unbounded delight, he left university to enter Parks Air College in East St. Louis, Illinois, at that time one of the most famed institutions of its kind in the United States. At Parks he studied every phase of flying, including navigation, meteorology, engines, air frames and instrument flying. In a wide variety of aircraft, from Stinson Reliants to Travelaires and Monocoupes, he built up enough experience to win his commercial pilot's license, and he was recognized at last as a qualified aviator by the United States government. In fact, the government gave him an extra stamp of approval by accepting him as a pilot in the 110th Observation Squadron of the Missouri National Guard, the outfit in which no less a celebrity than his boyhood hero, Charles A. Lindbergh, had once served.

There was never another thought of law after all this. Bill Vanderkloot was now firmly and happily married to his childhood sweetheart, a sometimes fickle jade who in her own fascinating way would lead him along many distant and adventurous pathways through the skies of the world.

Not that his first paid civilian job as a pilot was to be all that glamorous. One of his comrades in 110 Squadron happened to mention to him one day that a struggling air service operator named Clyde Brayton, who ran a small charter business out of a broken down building in a corner of Lambert Field in St. Louis, was looking for a pilot.

When Bill was accepted for the job, he soon learned that it wasn't just to fill a vacancy in the piloting staff. It was to *become* the flying staff, Brayton having no other pilot with his establishment but himself. The rest of the firm was made up of one girl Friday and Joe York, a welder-mechanic whose oft-repeated boast was that he could mend "anything but a broken heart." And there was indeed plenty to mend in keeping Clyde Brayton's aging aircraft aloft.

A big barrel-chested man with dark hair, bushy eyebrows and a shy and quiet manner, Brayton was immensely proud of the fact that he held pilot's license No. 12, which was right down there in the respected low numbers quite close to Lindbergh's. There had been lots of earlier fliers, but when the U.S. government first began to issue licenses to pilots, the process was started in the St. Louis area. Clyde and Lindbergh happened to be in that vicinity and were included among the low numbers.

But even if Clyde Brayton hadn't been a barnstorming contemporary of Lucky Lindy, Bill Vanderkloot still would have liked and admired greatly his first flying boss.

"He was a man of tremendous integrity," Bill later recalled. "There were plenty of times, in those lean periods, when Clyde had an awful time scraping together my $40 a week. I knew full well there wasn't anything left over in the till for himself after he'd paid off the rest of us."

On Bill's part, he did his best to give full value for wages received, and then some. The way it worked out, Clyde was president of the outfit and Bill became a kind of general manager, chief pilot, chief instructor and odd job man doing everything from selling sightseeing flights to curious visitors to helping push the aircraft into the hangars at the end of the day.

On the day before Christmas, 1937, Clyde Brayton, a rather reluctant man in the talking department, tried to express his feelings toward his keen young associate in the form of a Yuletide letter to him:

This is a note of genuine appreciation for the sincere effort, thought, careful hard work, and honesty you have put forth in helping make possible the operation that our company now has. I wish to go on record as saying that this is the first time since I've operated Brayton Flying Service, that I feel I have a right hand man and a first class assistant which I need not worry about in my absence from the city.

I can completely disregard operations at home when I go on trips that take me away from the city, because, I am positively certain things will be taken care of.

Your opportunities with this company are unlimited. The surface of our operations has only been scratched. With your ambition and honest effort, you will go a long way with us.

But it was all quite joyful and immensely satisfying work, seven days a week, for a young fellow who so loved flying. In all of Bill Vanderkloot's long and eventful flying career, he never enjoyed anything quite so much as he did those glorious days at Lambert Field. It was a period when, if anyone wanted to sit down around most airports, it was still necessary to find a handy oil or gas drum in the shade of a hangar.

In a comparatively few years, measured by the terms usually applied to the unfolding of history, men would be flying to the moon. But in the 1930s in St. Louis, there was still that rich and heady spice to flying. Aviation was growing up, but it was still in its early youth—brash, lusty and questionable as a means to fortune, yet full of camaraderie, adventure and dreams. Newer and more sophisticated instruments and other equipment were useful, of course, and eventually pointed the way for aviation to become a vast industry.

But there was a time, not so very long ago, when airmen could still gaze up toward the stars with a certain kind of innocent wonder. It was Bill Vanderkloot's great good fortune to spend some of that magic age pioneering with Clyde Brayton at Lambert Field.

Chapter Four

It may be barely possible that the same Providence which punishes man for his transgressions against man may also operate, somewhere in that Office in the Sky, a small back-room mechanical department which wreaks vengeance upon him who slights faithful, iron beasts of burden like Ford Model A roadsters. Henry Ford, who, it was said, believed in things like reincarnation, might have enjoyed a small chuckle over the fact that the high-sounding Air Boss, for which Bill had traded his Model A, had piled young Vanderkloot into a cypress swamp.

Almost equally mysterious were the events surrounding the arrival in 1938 of Bill Vanderkloot and his pal Mel Kassing in Kansas City in response to the acceptance of their applications to join a scheduled airline as apprentice pilots. After a year and a half with Clyde Brayton's small charter service, Bill had developed a yen to serve on a regular airline and it was with high and eager expectations that he and Kassing reached Kansas City ready to report for duty.

They were so excited about their prospects that when they drew up in front of the hotel, after driving together from St. Louis in Bill's brand new car, they rushed right in to register without bothering to haul out their luggage. When they returned to the street to collect their baggage, their car had disappeared with all of their other belongings and was never seen by them again.

By this time Bill Vanderkloot had about 1,500 hours of flying time under his belt and had just gained his Airline Transport Rating. But weeks of study at the airline pilots' school passed before he was judged ready to climb into the right hand seat of a DC-2 on his initial flight as a first officer, on the run from Kansas City to Albuquerque, New Mexico.

There weren't any oversold seats or waiting lists on airline flights in those days. A heavy passenger load on the Kansas City-Albuquerque run might amount to no more than five or six white-knuckled wayfarers.

Meteorological services were sketchy, and as is still the practice, the final decision on whether a flight would leave or not rested upon the captain—except when weather reports were considered and out-weighed, as sometimes happened then, by the amount of freight and the number of passengers that were ready to go. In other words, two paying passengers and slightly questionable weather might delay a flight a little longer than a full load of passengers and moderately threatening weather.

There was at this time, of course, little opportunity to climb above the weather as can be done now by the haughty jets. A pilot either had to go through it or around it. If he chose to go through it, he sometimes had to wring out his soggy uniform at the end of the line. For some strange reason, the DC-2's were designed so that, although the passengers always remained fairly dry in a rainstorm, the pilot and co-pilot seemed relatively exposed to the elements. The flight deck had a tendency to be plagued around the windows and the ceiling by various kinds of leaky seams through which the rain sometimes dripped and trickled in miserable fashion.

Such weather advice as did exist was based mainly on "spot information," meaning the local conditions which happened to prevail at that moment at various stations along the route. The kind of weather which lay between these distant points—including roving thunderheads of extremely erratic and ugly moods—could only be guessed at.

Navigational aids were similarly sketchy, consisting mainly of widely separated radio range stations which sometimes grew fickle and coy at the very moment when you needed them most. More than once Bill Vanderkloot and his captain had to double check their radio-aided navigation by studying, down below, the meandering but more reliable "iron compass" provided by the railway line between Kansas City and Albuquerque.

"If you see any cows or chickens running away on the starboard side," remarked Bill's skipper casually one muggy day, "we're quite a bit off course."

With great mock solemnity, he then took the pains to explain to his rookie first officer that the bored cows and chickens who didn't dash about helter-skelter as the DC-2 passed overhead obviously resided on farms lying directly below the correct and fairly regular flight path from Kansas City to Albuquerque.

The vagaries of the weather and the scanty meteorological resources with which to keep track of its everchanging moods sometimes resulted in peculiar incidents.

One evening, for instance, an encounter with increasingly bad weather finally caused a flight to be grounded in Fort Wayne, Indiana. The passengers didn't object much when they were told the flight was not proceeding any farther or when they were loaded into buses to continue the journey to their destinations by highway. Such frustrations were fairly common in the early days of airline operations. Bill Vanderkloot and his captain took a taxicab to a small, nearby hotel. In the morning, the captain rolled around in his bed and rubbing his eyes sleepily, peered glumly for a moment out the window. All was bleak and grey.

"Well, that's that," he remarked with a grateful yawn. "We sure won't be flying this morning in that kind of stuff."

He then went back to blissful slumber. But not for long. In a few minutes he was awakened rudely by the jangle of the telephone. The call was from the flight superintendent in Chicago wanting to know when the

25

aircraft would be departing from Fort Wayne in accordance with the previous night's instructions to ferry it to Chicago where it was badly needed, if and when the weather cleared in the morning.

"We're desperate for that aircraft and I expected it would be here long ago," testily complained the super.

"There's no way we can get out of here this morning," said the captain. "The weather is right down on the deck."

"That's mighty funny," replied the puzzled super. "I've just been talking to the Met boys at Fort Wayne and they tell me the weather there is bright, sunny and perfectly CAVU!"

Putting down the telephone, the startled and now wide-awake captain padded over to the window and took another, harder look. This time he made the disconcerting discovery that the window of their hotel room was located about three feet from the grey brick wall of an adjacent building. Overhead, the sky was clear and blue! Bill and his embarrassed skipper were soon dressed and dashing off for the Fort Wayne airport.

One thing Bill Vanderkloot learned quite early in his airline apprenticeship was that the DC-2 was hardly what might be called a co-pilot's airplane. On the contrary, it sometimes seemed to have been expressly designed by the Douglas Aircraft Company for the sole and evil purpose of testing possible future captains so severely that the chaff could be separated from the grain long before the airline had wasted too much much money on the trying of them.

One of the first officer's duties, for example, was to raise and lower manually the DC-2's heavy landing gear and wing flaps by means of levers which had to be pumped vigorously from their position between his seat and that of the captain. Give or take a pump or two, it took fifty-seven pushes and retractions of one lever to raise or lower the wheels. If the first officer happened to be on a run which had many intermediate stops, he ended up in a most pitiful state of exhaustion at the end of the route.

26

"On this airline," one of his fellow pilots confided to Bill, "you can always tell the first officers from the captains without ever bothering to look at their sleeve stripes. A first officer is always much more highly developed muscularly on his left side. And when he climbs down out of the cockpit, he is usually sweaty and bedraggled, with his tongue hanging out, while the cool and debonair captain steps forth looking every inch the fashion plate!"

"Dead head," or empty runs, were fairly common at that time, when the scanty equipment affordable in those lean days of airline operations had to be shuffled about constantly to maintain schedules. Sometimes on such runs, pilots were pleased to have the monotony broken by the presence of a fresh and interesting stewardess just on her way to take up her new duties. All candidates for stewardess jobs then had to be registered nurses and mighty good looking.

On such occasions, one crew in their DC-3 sometimes indulged in a little diversion which never failed to enliven a long no-passenger run. Up on the flight deck was a length of rubber hose with a kind of nozzle on the end of it which was used to blow a powerful stream of warm air against the windshield to remove from it some of the moisture fog which gathered there under certain conditions. The automatic pilot was coming into use then and, after setting up the course on "George," as this device was called, the captain and co-pilot would extract from its special storage place a black rubber glove kept there for just such times. The nozzle was removed from the end of the air hose and in its place they secured with rubber bands the wrist portion of the glove. The air caused it to balloon out with amazingly realistic and creepy twitchings of the inflated thumb and fingers. This eerie hand they then placed on the control wheel. Next, they lowered as for jumping purposes the two side windows of the cockpit, and then crawled into the nearby port and starboard baggage compartments. Just before closing the door the last man in rang for the stewardess.

When the young lady obediently came dashing up

to answer the always respected summons from the flight deck, the sight she encountered caused many a spilled cup of coffee; although, curiously enough, no case exists on record of a new stewardess actually swooning in flight or submitting her resignation from the line immediately after touchdown.

There were, of course, many more chances for such horseplay aloft in those early days when the airlines were in the fledgling stage. There was the case of the captain with a strange sense of humor who liked to take advantage of the peculiar fact that the aisle of a DC-2 always slanted down somewhat toward the tail even when the aircraft was flying straight and level. It was his whim to extract, from a store he always carried in his pocket, a handful of loose nuts and bolts which he stealthily would place on the floor behind him. Propelled by gravity and vibration, they would roll down gradually along the aisle past the seats of the horrified passengers.

Today's airliners and their crews are much more sophisticated and devoid of nonsense. Even trusty George has become so educated and refined that it is now possible for an automatic pilot to take a Boeing 747 right down through the thickest overcast to a perfect landing on the runway without ever requiring the controls to be touched by human hands. It would hardly be an exaggeration to say that not all airline pilots are wildly enthusiastic about such scientific marvels. A veteran skipper recently expressed it quite succinctly, "I have no desire to go sliding, blindfold, down an electronic bannister at 150 knots with a twenty-million dollar corporation strapped to my ass!"

But in those distant days, the hearts of most airline pilots were as young and gay as their pocketbooks were lean. As a probationary co-pilot, Bill Vanderkloot made a little more than $200 a month. He shared an apartment with his fellow pilot Mel Kassing, and so delicate were their combined economic resources that when Mel got married, Bill had to stay right on with the bride and groom. He didn't have enough money to rent an apartment of his own, and if he did move out the newlyweds could no longer afford the apartment they were already in.

One day early in 1941, after concluding a flight into New York's LaGuardia Airport, Bill Vanderkloot and a couple of other airline pilots were walking through a hangar when they encountered a new and most impressive sight.

Standing there on the wide hangar floor was one of the biggest and sleekest airplanes they had ever seen. The immense four-engined bomber, on its way to the war in Europe, looked to them like some kind of aerial giant, after the comparatively tiny DC-2s and DC-3s they had been flying. The huge machine was bound for Britain from the Long Beach, California, factory of the Consolidated Vultee Aircraft Corporation where it had been built. It already bore the proud red, white and blue rondels of the Royal Air Force painted on its sides and wings.

The second of its kind to come off the production line, the great bomber was of a type designated technically as a Consolidated B-24. When it joined the strength of the RAF, this particular aircraft was known as *Liberator* AL504. But eventually it would become better known, the world over, simply as the *Commando*.

Although he never dreamt of such a thing, as he and his fellow pilots admiringly ran their hands and eyes over this giant aerial man-o'-war that day at LaGuardia, Bill Vanderkloot had a date with it and with destiny. It would be a rendez-vous so strange and unbelievable that on many a dark night, in far-off and dangerous skies, he would sit at the controls of that very airplane, wondering what on earth or in the high heavens a young fellow from Lake Bluff, Illinois, was doing up there.

Chapter Five

L iberator AL504's stopover at LaGuardia Airport was her last pause in the United States on the long journey to Great Britain from the California plant of Consolidated Vultee. From New York the big aircraft would proceed to Dorval Airport near Montreal, then on to Gander Airport in Newfoundland and thence on the final and longest hop across the North Atlantic to Prestwick, Scotland. Such was the usual route from the U.S. production lines to the European theatre of war.

This might not be considered today a particularly hazardous or adventurous voyage, in an era when so many air passengers board a flight bound across the North Atlantic almost as casually as they might set out from New York to Chicago or from Toronto to Montreal. But it might be useful to place the story of Bill Vanderkloot and *Liberator* AL504 in proper perspective with a brief description of the state of the highly dangerous and delicate art of flying across an ocean as it existed in 1941. Of all the seas of the world which might humble the audacious men who set out to conquer them on relatively flimsy wings, none was so mean and vindictive as that wide and forever cold expanse of water called the North Atlantic. And at no time was the North Atlantic in a crueler, more vengeful mood, on its surface or in the misty skies above it, than in the grey and dismal months of winter.

At the outbreak of the Second World War in 1939, it was considered sheer folly to attempt a winter aerial crossing of the North Atlantic. Its cloud cover was seething then with super-cooled water droplets which could turn quickly into murderous layers of ice—on wings, propellers and tail surfaces—ice that could press an aircraft down into the sea like a giant and relentless hand. Often, with the kind of aircraft available, it was impossible to climb above this cruel and frigid shroud which sometimes hung so low over the waves that there was no safe way under it, either.

Even by 1941, weather forecasting for aviation on the North Atlantic was of such a primitive nature that those meteorologists who were rash enough to attempt it were still looked upon as only slightly scientific voodoo men, or mad yogis with eyes pitifully blurred from gazing too long into crystal balls.

There were no radio beams or regular enroute weather reports and little chance of rescue should an aircraft be forced down upon this vast, treacherous and frigid sea.

In the early stage of the war, long-range military aircraft manufactured in North America had to be transported to Britain aboard ships, taking up precious cargo space on the vital and desperately maintained convoy route well-named the Atlantic Lifeline.

But, as has happened more than once under the urgency and stress of war, bold men were spurred to take bold measures. In the early months of 1940, the principal shipments of aircraft to Britain from the United States consisted of twin-engined Lockhead Hudsons, badly needed overseas by the Royal Air Force Coastal Command to patrol the submarine-infested shipping lanes on the approaches to Britain.

Transporting these aircraft as deck cargo on the slow moving and constantly harrassed ships of the Atlantic convoys meant a time lapse of roughly three months between the final test flight of a new Hudson in the United States and its entry into service with an operational squadron in Great Britain. It was estimated that if these aircraft could only be *flown* across the Atlantic, the time lag from the final U.S. test flight to patrol service off the British coast could be cut to as

31

little as ten days. Not only that, the aircraft, instead of being bulky cargo, could themselves become cargo carriers, speeding desperately needed, small but vital weapons and other equipment across the sea to hard-pressed Britain.

The British government in 1940 discussed the feasibility of such a project with G. H. Woods-Humphery, former managing director of Imperial Airways, forerunner of the present British Airways. Woods-Humphery believed it could be done, both in summer and winter. Two important decisions followed shortly thereafter: one was to try the wild-sounding scheme as soon as possible; and the other was to set up headquarters for the ferry service in Montreal, under the supervision of what was then called the Air Services Department of the Canadian Pacific Railway.

The matter of attempting the great gamble was actually settled, in its broad and basic form, by two old and titled friends, both Canadians who had pursued highly distinguished careers on opposite sides of the Atlantic. One was the dynamic Lord Beaverbrook, publisher of the *London Daily Express,* who was serving then as Britain's Minister of Aircraft Production. The other was Sir Edward Beatty, Chairman and President of the Canadian Pacific Railway, one of the largest transportation systems in the world, which had a vast amount of experience in moving passengers and freight upon the sea, and the land and to a smaller extent at the time, in the air.

Woods-Humphery was sent out to Canada to assist the C.P.R.'s Air Services Department in setting up the new organization. He brought with him a well tried group of old Imperial Airways hands. They included Captains A.A. Wilcockson, D.C.T. Bennett, I.C. Ross, R. Humphrey Page and Colonel H. Burchall. Another member of this initial group was a particularly hard-bitten former Imperial Airways skipper named G. J. (Taffy) Powell, who had served as a Squadron Leader in the R.A.F. He was one of the pilots who in those early days had helped pioneer the Imperial Airways overseas summer routes across the Atlantic in flying boats, by way of the Azores and Bermuda.

Later, a famed Canadian war ace and bush pilot named C.H. (Punch) Dickins would take over the direction of these ferry services, as head of the Air Services Department of the C.P.R. He had participated in a number of aviation "firsts" (including the first airmail flights into the Arctic) and was to serve with great distinction in this bold new enterprise.

The original western terminus of the Atlantic ferry operation was established at St. Hubert Airport near Montreal. From there the planes would be flown to a rather crude and hastily enlarged airport being developed near Gander Lake in Newfoundland. From Gander the aircraft would set off on the final, long and hazardous flight across the North Atlantic. (Gander would become eventually a kind of aerial crossroads of the world, until the high-flying and far-ranging jets, able to proceed directly from the North American mainland to Europe, made the Newfoundland stopover unnecessary and Gander obsolete. But on the cold evening of November 10, 1940, Gander was still a rough and rugged slash in the Newfoundland wilderness, with many exciting days and nights still ahead of it.)

Lined up that evening on the tarmac at Gander were seven Hudson bombers which had been flown there by civilian pilots in the employ of the Lockheed Aircraft Company.

The great idea was that the aircraft, all but one of which were being flown by C.P.R. ferry crews with little or no experience in over-ocean navigation, would fly in a close formation led by the Imperial Airways veteran Captain Bennett. Keeping in contact by wireless telegraph the crews would depend heavily on him for moral support and navigational advice during the journey.

At the takeoff hour, amidst the forest and the gust-driven snow and the feebly floodlit darkness of Gander Airport, there occurred one small but noble salute to the fact that history was being made that night. As Captain Bennett, in the leading Hudson, gunned its motors for takeoff, he all but drowned out the wavering strains of *There'll Always Be An England,* played by a brave little military band assembled near the runway. One after the other, with a lapse of only ten minutes between the departure of the first and seventh Hudsons, the bombers rolled down the runway and climbed into the darkness over the Atlantic. The blue flames from the exhaust ports of their twin 1,100 h.p. Wright Cyclone engines fitfully broke the sullen gloom as the planes disappeared eastward into the night, on this first ferrying attempt. Somewhere out there they might meet the dawn and hopefully sight, not long afterward, the glorious landfall that would mean the hard part of this audacious venture was over.

The fine idea of staying in formation and allowing the one fully experienced ocean-flying hand to do the navigation and act as mother hen for all didn't work out as well as had been expected. Captain Bennett later described the problem. "It was a dark night," he said, "and the weather enroute was rather a mixed bag—as one might expect on such a long leg. With the help of formation flight the whole group managed to stay with me, in spite of passing through broken cloud layers. Eventually, however, we had the bad luck to run into the top of a very virile warm front, and we were forced to break formation at 18,000 feet and to spread out to avoid collision. I went up, but I was still in quite heavy snow and turbulence at 20,000 feet, so all had to continue on their own."

If Captain Bennett's terse description of such a potentially disastrous foul-up in the careful plan sounds rather casual, it must be remembered that it came from a seasoned and utterly unflappable Imperial Airways skipper. At the very moment that he was attempting to lead his confused flock on this epic flight, he was sitting in the left hand seat of his Hudson, his black homburg hat meticulously stowed in the cockpit and his inevitable briefcase sitting neatly at his side. (After all, it was Captain Bennett, the perfectionist, who one evening in a Montreal nightclub while

34

his companions were talking about women, was discovered with a stopwatch on the table, counting the number of persons passing by and scientifically clocking their rate of progress, which was sometimes remarkably slow and wavering as they moved to and from the washrooms.)

Radio Officer C.M. (Curly) Tripp, riding in Hudson T-9468 piloted by Captain Ralph E. Adams with Flying Officer Dana Gentry as co-pilot, was less reserved in his record of the historic trip.

For the first hour there seemed to be planes all around us, and which one was the leader was the question. Ralph turned over to Dana and with the torch began to check over the ship and found oil leaking badly from the starboard tank. I passed a message to the leader, Captain Bennett, that our oil tank had ruptured but we were watching closely and would keep him advised. Our Skipper, being in some doubt as to whether to go on or not, held back.

Finally he decided the oil flow was diminishing; and after deciding to go on, we found ourselves quite alone. Then my radio blew up by shorting in the antenna switch box and giving us all a good scare.

Ralph shouted, "Turn the damned thing off!" but I had beat him to the gun. With that load of gas it isn't pleasant to have fire skipping around the cockpit, and the corona from that transmitter was really something.

When the skipper decided to go on, we climbed up to 16,000 feet, which afterward proved a smart move as we gained on the rest right from there. At 00.14 G.M.T., Captain Bennett figured his position at Lat. 50.58 N, Long. 48.38 W.

I will always appreciate Adams' friendly advice to forget the radio for awhile, as we were pretty high and it was no use tiring myself out. What with the excitement of the takeoff and the leaking oil tank, I was glad to sit back and relax and I think I actually enjoyed myself. When I look back now I can't feel that I was actually relaxing, but at the time it felt good just to sit there and try not to think of anything. If Ralph and Dana were doing the same thing, we all snapped out of it at 02.07 when our bomb bay tank ran dry and both motors started cutting out.

I was not expecting it, and even if Ralph and Dana were, the way they went for that hand pump and gas valve made me think they didn't like it any better than I did. I don't think anything ever sounded so good to me as hearing those big Wrights hit their stride again and settle down to a steady drone. From then on the Skipper didn't have to watch any gauges. I could tell him every minute how much gas was left in whatever tank he was on. He got quite a kick out of this and I took some kidding afterwards, Dana calling me the "human gas gauge."

At 02.03, while I was trying to take a bearing on Captain Bennett, the indicator on the radio compass broke and I felt really up the creek without a paddle. No transmitter or radio compass and out over the Atlantic Ocean! I didn't have the heart to tell Ralph the compass was on the bum, but from then on I couldn't sit there doing nothing, so I asked permission to go to work on the transmitter.

At 03.40, G.M.T., we were at 18,000 feet, and we must have looked funny sitting there with rubber tubes stuck in our mouths. I sometimes get scared when I think of how we started out that first trip with one little tank of oxygen and nothing but a rubber tube to suck it through. Ralph did the regulating and knew what he was doing. None of us suffered any ill effects, although at one time I felt my stomach would cave in and Ralph got down in the nose and had trouble getting up . . . .

At 03.40 I felt very pleased to be able to tell the Skipper we had a transmitter again and I think it was a load off his mind, although he said nothing.

At 04.40 Captain Bennett reported Long. 24.50 W. and we knew we were doing well too. Gentry was a treasure, the way he fooled around as though we were just on a pleasant jaunt and didn't have a care in the world. The one thing I won't ever forget is the look we had together at the full moon through the Astro hatch. It was a beautiful and awe-inspiring sight, and made us realize what a very small part of the world one really is.

At 05.00 the Captain spotted what appeared to be a light on our starboard bow, and Columbus himself could not have looked more longingly at North America than we did at that light. We were sure it was one of the other planes, and when it proved to be a star, we couldn't help but feel a bit let down. The Skipper had been losing altitude. When we couldn't get contact at 2,000 feet, he pulled back up to 6,000 and stayed there. We were in rain cloud off and on; after the cold of 18,000 feet, we were

forced to take off our heavy clothing as it was quite warm
. . . .

All was quiet on air, as we were keeping W/T silence east of 20 degrees west. Control was trying to pass Met. traffic but no one could read him through the rain static. Once W/T silence was broken, it was a wild scramble. The Skipper casually mentioned that he could use a bearing but after listening to the static, realized it was hopeless.

At 08.00 we started to descend, and at 5,000 feet came contact. Dana was down in the nose, and I don't know who was the most surprised when he casually stuck his head up and said, "Say, Captain, there's land down there!" It was a big moment. Ralph stuck her nose down to get a better look and reached for the map case. . . . We were over land, but there was water in the distance. It was a tense moment when Ralph pointed to a little spot on the map and said, "That's it over there, Catlin Island." It didn't take long to prove him right.

It was only a few minutes until we came over Lough Neagh, which was really beautiful in the morning light. Suddenly the Captain let out a roar and shouted, "There's Aldergrove right over there!" With that he shoved the throttles forward and the way that Hudson jumped was like a horse coming down the home stretch. After one circuit we were down, at 08.50, G.M.T. We were third in. . . ."

That sight greatly pleased, but by no means relaxed, Captain Bennett, who was standing in the R.A.F. station with his face glued to the window, waiting for the straggled arrival of the other maiden ocean-pilots who had started out in such hopeful formation, and might now be God knew where.

He was looking for a miracle, and he got it. Slightly more than ten hours out of Gander, the last of those seven wandering Hudsons, incredible as it was, finally came winging down out the skies of Northern Ireland and safely rolled to a halt on the runway at Aldergrove near Belfast.

When the weary crews—twenty-two unshaven men; nine of them Americans, six British, six Canadians and one Australian—were at last safely assembled in the R.A.F. mess, the impeccable Captain Bennett, looking tidily clean of chin, donned his black homburg hat at an unusually rakish angle and opened his brief-case. He carefully extracted from its depths twenty-two bright-red paper poppies, which he had confidently purchased in Montreal only a few days before. These he proceeded to hand out to the bedraggled men who had so dramatically and successfully helped him prove that the bombers which would eventually achieve supremacy in the skies of Europe could be flown across the North Atlantic at all seasons. It was a nice touch, on that chilly morning in Aldergrove, on November 11, 1940, the twenty-second anniversary of what was called Armistice Day of the war that was supposed to end all wars.

It was revealed later that had this first North Atlantic ferry attempt not been so amazingly successful the whole project might have been abandoned. Those who set the plan in motion had been prepared to continue it if a minimum of three of those first seven aircraft arrived safely in Britain. When all of them managed to make it, despite their wanderings and stragglings from the original formation, Lord Beaverbrook and other members of his department concluded that the seemingly hare-brained scheme did have a great deal of merit.

Only three more formation flights were attempted from Gander to Aldergrove, the trouble being that the planes could start out in fairly good formation, but they could never reach the other side of the Atlantic that way. Although none was permanently lost, the Hudsons invariably became separated along the way, some being forced to land at other scattered airports in Ireland or Scotland, rather than Aldergrove, the one they were heading for.

Having one or two qualified celestial navigators riding in "mother hen" ships in the formation to guide the inexperienced crews of the other aircraft had seemed originally like a great plan, but it just didn't work.

Remarked Imperial Airways Captain W. L. (Geordie) Stewart, who led one of these formation flights, "Formation flying, even in decent conditions in daylight, is quite an art. At night, with no navigation lights, it's more than that. . . . As it was you had people coming over the top of you and people coming underneath you. Why they never hit each other I've never been able to understand. In formation flying you've got to anticipate all the time in three dimensions. To do it at night with all the rest of the people never having had any experience, is hair-raising."

Some of the later wayfarers in the long hop across the North Atlantic would find it was also a bit hair-raising, at times, to be hanging up there in the sky above the angry waves in a tiny three-man world that seemed so ridiculously fragile and alone among the immense and surly elements which surrounded it. The slightest hesitation in the steady snore of the Wright Cyclones sounded like a deadly snort indeed, and a word of advice from some leader, even in the thin and stuttering voice of the wireless telegraph, could provide heavenly comfort in more ways than one.

Despite these comforts, formation flights were forsaken. Pilots flew in solitary aircraft; the miracle is that so many survived and learned how to fly this way so well.

They made a peculiar collection, the old hands and the new engaged in flying those bombers across the formidable North Atlantic. A few of the tenderfeet sometimes received tremendous scares when the Germans began sending long-range Focke-Wolfe Condor aircraft as far out as they could reach into the Atlantic from their European bases to garner information on the weather. These weather planes had been relieved of every unrequired ounce in order to fly as far as possible westward over the Atlantic, leaving sufficient fuel to return. This stripping of weight included armaments. The aircraft weren't intended for combat. Their sole purpose was to observe and report the weather, which usually approached Europe on the prevailing winds from the west.

This was all very well except that a German plane was still a German plane and on more than one occasion, near the end of a long and tiring flight across the Atlantic, the startled crew of a Britain-bound Hudson, also unarmed to save weight, would be severely shocked to gaze out in the half-light of daybreak to see a Luftwaffe weather plane flying almost off their wingtips. Such occasions, though by no means everyday occurrences, had the effect, when they did happen of putting a weary ferry crew so smartly and alertly back on their toes that they probably would have flown the rest of the way in a rigid, standing position had this awkward posture been possible within the cramped nose cockpit of a Hudson.

Among the oldtimers who helped deliver the growing armada of bombers to Britain, none was more jaunty and confident that the redoubtable Captain O. P. Jones, a veteran Imperial Airways hand. In the days of peace following the war, he would continue his ocean-hopping career as a senior and highly respected skipper with B.O.A.C.; and would, in 1951, fly the future Queen Elizabeth and her husband Prince Phillip on their first visit to Canada. O.P. Jones sported a saucy, close-clipped, pointed beard, long before this type of facial adornment became so popular, giving him a kind of Sir Walter Raleigh look. When, in 1951, he performed a gallant and courtly bow beside the red carpet at Dorval, the modern Elizabeth shook his hand and thanked him for her safe journey across the Atlantic in the Boeing Stratocruiser under his command. This historical replay did not escape the notice of the news reporters.

It was, indeed, the imperturbable O. P. Jones who so deftly quelled the momentary terror of his crew mates aboard a Britain-bound bomber one night with a remark which is generally conceded to be one of the more classic moments in the annals of Ferry Command. A companion on the flight deck that night later described the incident as follows:

> Midway across, on one occasion, the light at the instrument panel failed. The second pilot, making his first Atlantic flight, was at the controls at the time, and Captain Jones had retired to the engineer's position to write up his logbook by the glow from the dials on that panel.

Flight Engineer Stack made way for him, and sat down on the floor to eat an apple.

At that moment, over the middle of the Atlantic, all four engines cut out simultaneously. It transpired later that the pilot, adjusting the automatic controls in darkness, had accidently pulled the master switch for all engines. They were then at about 14,000 feet, and they glided rapidly to 6,000 feet before the captain, striding forward, had remedied the mishap and brought the engines to life again. But before he did so, he closed his logbook with some deliberation, laid his pen down beside it, turned to the engineer, and casually remarked, "Strangely quiet in here, *isn't* it, Mr. Stack?"

Chapter Six

In January of 1941, just a few weeks before First Officer Bill Vanderkloot was to qualify for his long dreamed of promotion to an airline captaincy and a command of his own, he was approached during a layover in New York by a representative of an organization called the Clayton Knight Commission. The proposition he had to offer was a most fascinating and attractive one. He was recruiting civilian pilots in the United States for what had become by then the Royal Air Force Ferry Command.

Ferry Command, with headquarters in Montreal, was offering the astronomical pay of $1,000 a month in tax free U.S. funds to American civilian pilots.

Despite the imminence of his hard-earned appointment as an airline captain, Bill Vanderkloot found the temptation of joining Ferry Command too great. Here was a chance for high adventure and the sight of distant and glamorous places—plus a salary that was more than four times the one he was receiving at that time. It took him only about two hours from the time of the interview for him to make his big decision.

Three days later he was off to Montreal. His instructions were to report, on his arrival, to the Canadian Pacific Air Services Department on Craig Street.

When the official business of presenting himself for duty was finished, he loaded his scant baggage into a taxi and proceeded according to orders to the Mount Royal Hotel. This was the main lodging place and socializing centre for the highly interesting assortment of adventurers who had been mustered from all over the world to fly the evergrowing streams of bombers across the Atlantic. On the ground floor of the Mount Royal was a popular watering hole known as the Piccadilly Club, all red drapes and leather chairs, where at various hours enough off-duty Ferry Command pilots could be found to man at least a squadron or two of Britain-bound aircraft.

It was there that Bill Vanderkloot struck up one of his early Ferry Command friendships with another recruit named C. A. ("Duke") Schiller. Although Schiller, who was sometimes called "Foghorn Duke," hailed originally from the United States, where he had driven speedboats for Gar Wood, he had been flying in the Canadian bush country for so long that he had already become a legend in the northern wilderness.

Among his more spectacular exploits had been his flight in 1928, through blinding snowstorms, to rescue the crew of the Junkers aircraft *Bremen* after it had crash-landed on lonely Greenly Island, in the Strait of Belle Isle, at the end of an historic 37-hour, east-to-west flight across the North Atlantic from Dublin, Ireland. It was flown by the German pilots Captain Herman Koehl and Baron Von Huenfeld and an Irishman named Colonel James Fitzmaurice.

Schiller and Vanderkloot were to make a rather oddly matched pair of buddies. Bill was inclined to be a rather modest type of fellow, fairly serious and soft-spoken. Duke, on the other hand, was a loud and boisterous man who had won the extra appellation of Foghorn quite honestly.

Sometimes the Ferry Command inmates of the Piccadilly Club wondered whether a spy might be lurking at some nearby table straining his ears to overhear their conversations. In the case of Duke Schiller, such close-range intelligence operations wouldn't have been at all necessary. It was quite possible for a secret agent to sit right out in his car on Peel Street in front of the Mount Royal Hotel and hear with perfect clarity Duke Schiller's remarks from deep inside the Piccadilly Club.

Most of his fellow pilots agreed that Duke Schiller was no bashful mumbler or whisperer. But they were also nearly unanimous on at least two other matters: that Duke Schiller could drink an awful lot of whiskey; and that he was one of the best "seat-of-the-pants" pilots who ever sat at the controls of an airplane. Some of them even suspected that underneath Duke Schiller's long-handled underwear his skin was probably covered with feathers. Such awesome respect was quite unusual among pilots discussing their peers.

Together and at about the same rate of progress, Duke Schiller and Bill Vanderkloot completed the first stage of their initiation into Ferry Command which sufficiently familiarized them with the operation of Lockheed Hudson bombers. These still made up the bulk of the machines being flown across the Atlantic at that time.

It didn't take either of them long to get the hang of the strange aircraft, during practice sessions at the newly opened airport at Dorval, near Montreal. Dorval had by then replaced St. Hubert as the western terminus of the Atlantic ferry route when swelling Ferry Command traffic made it necessary to develop a new and larger airport in what had been a race track and surrounding expanse of farmland at Dorval. These meadows were eventually to become what is now Montreal's great and bustling international airport.

Being at Dorval during the day and ofttimes in the Mount Royal's jolly Piccadilly Club at night, Bill Vanderkloot began to recognize more and more, as the weeks passed by, that in joining Ferry Command he had become part of the most colourful and in many ways most incredible band of aerial adventurers ever to be gathered into one single organization. Looking back upon it now, it would be reasonably safe to say that it was the most fantastic one of its kind that ever *will* be mustered. They were the last of a vanishing breed.

Of approximately 425 aircrew members who were flying the bombers across the Atlantic at that time, about fifty-nine per cent of the pilots were Americans;

twenty-eight per cent were from the United Kingdom; ten per cent were Canadians; and three per cent were of other nationalities.

Of these, about half—including most of the pilots from the still officially neutral United States—were civilians. The other half consisted of uniformed members of the various British Commonwealth and Allied air forces.

The military pilots received the straight and quite modest air force pay of about one pound a day, compared to the $1,000-per-month salaries of the civilians. Some of the military pilots groused about this inequality of the pay checks. But others shrugged it off in the comforting knowledge that they and their fellow officers were carrying out their risky chores with a certain amount of financial protection provided by their governments for both them and their families. If they should lose their lives, at least a small provision would be made for their dependents. If they should be forced down and captured in enemy territory, their pay would continue while they were being held prisoners.

The civilian pilots, on the other hand, were strictly on their own. No death benefits, no pensions, no prisoner of war pay. At least one civilian pilot, who wandered off course and was captured, spent more than two years in a prison camp during which time neither he nor his family received a penny from the government. The moment he made his forced landing in German-occupied France, he was no longer employed by the R.A.F.F.C. This condition was stipulated in the contract he had signed; along with the advice that during trips on duty away from his base of operations he would be allowed expenses of $8 per day for lodging and meals—provided that it was necessary for him to dine in restaurants and sleep in hotels. While riding in conveyances which provided some food and/or a place to grab a nap, the travelling allowance was cut to $4 a day.

The American civilian pilots made up a most curiously assorted lot. Most of them were highly qualified professional fliers, some from the barnstorming trade, some from the airlines, and some from the crop-dusting business, grown tired of hopping between the hedgerows and keen to see the sights of wartime London. And some recruits were just ardent adventurers with unusual gall who tried to bluff about their flying experience with cooked-up log books and who were weeded out quickly on their first check-flights.

The civilian pilots, who were not at that time required to wear uniforms, flew in a wide and fascinating variety of costumes. Some of the Texans, of whom there were a large number, wore high-heeled boots and ten-gallon hats. It was fairly easy to distinguish them from the British ferry pilots, with their stiff upper lips sometimes adorned by the striking handle-bar R.A.F. mustaches, then much in vogue in that gallant branch of His Majesty's Services.

Later on, fearing what might happen to some of its pilots if they were forced to land in enemy territory wearing civilian garb and were taken captive as spies, the ferrying service allowed them to don military uniforms—any kind of uniforms, so long as they were uniforms. At first, the rather casual instructions concerning the wearing of uniforms resulted in the blossoming forth of some peculiar military attire among those of more showy tastes. Former crop-dusters, barnstormers and stunt pilots suddenly turned up on their flight decks wearing such eye-catching ensembles as cowboy boots, ten-gallon hats and uniforms sporting generals' stars, crowns and other impressive symbols of rank. Finally, when Ferry Command became more organized and changed its name to Transport Command, civilian aircrews acquired standard uniforms of navy blue, similar to those worn in such organizations as Imperial Airways.

The ranks of Ferry Command included several noblemen representing the Free French forces and a number of pilots from the Free Polish Air Force. One former member of the Cuban Air Force wore on the breast of his tunic a particularly dazzling array of military decorations.

One evening in the Piccadilly Club, he explained

with great imitation solemnity, some of these honors to his awed and curious Ferry Command comrades. "This one," said he, "is for flying *high* across the entire *length* of Cuba. This one is for flying *high* across the entire *width* of Cuba. This one is for flying *diagonally* across Cuba. This one is for flying *low* across the entire *length* of Cuba, and this one is for flying *low* across the entire *width* of Cuba."

One of the most colorful of all that swashbuckling band was Charles ("Whitey") Dahl, an American who early in the war had come up to Canada to join the Royal Canadian Air Force. Whitey had already flown for the Loyalist side during the Spanish Civil War and had been shot down and captured by the rebel forces, after which he was tried and sentenced to death before a firing squad.

Receiving the news of Whitey's upcoming execution, some of his old barnstorming buddies back in the United States promptly set out to rescue him. They arranged with Edith Rogers, a quite stunning model and night club performer—who had never set eyes on Whitey Dahl—to write to General Francisco Franco a heart-rending appeal for the release of her beloved "husband." Whitey's pals, collaborating with this beautiful blonde, composed a letter that was a real tearjerker and sent it to Franco, along with her most glamorous pinup portrait.

The General fully measured up to the optimistic expectations of Whitey's scheming allies back in the United States by reacting the way a gallant Latin gentleman with a good eye for feminine charms is supposed to react. He released Whitey and sent him back to what he romantically supposed were the eager arms of his devoted and lovely wife. Later, after he returned to the United States, Whitey did meet this model a few times, in a casual way; but there is no record of them ever having seriously set up housekeeping.

At any rate, it worked out quite well for all concerned. Whitey didn't have to go to the wall in the yard of a Spanish prison, his stand-in "wife" won reams of valuable publicity in newspapers all over the world, and Franco was given credit for not allowing his political beliefs to entirely obscure the really important things of life. Back in the U.S., Edith's night club act was promptly billed "She Stopped The Firing Squad."

Although Whitey, as a Flight Lieutenant, received only the niggardly military pay of an R.C.A.F. officer in Ferry Command, he didn't complain about it much. Instead, he had the peculiar gift of making up for such injustices in many highly ingenious and enterprising ways.

His golden opportunity, if such an expression can be used, finally arrived when he was placed in charge of a small RA.F. emergency base in Para Belem, Brazil, after a South Atlantic ferry route had been established for Africa-bound aircraft. It seems he was doing extremely well down there at his lonely station in South America until Air Chief Marshal Sir Frederick Bowhill, head of the Royal Air Force Ferry Command, flew south from Montreal on one of his periodic inspection tours and happened to stop in at Whitey Dahl's almost forgotten outpost.

The legend is that the only reason Sir Frederick's plane was able to land at the station was that Whitey had not yet figured out any handy and profitable way to dispose of the concrete runways. Just about everything that was more portable on the base had been peddled long since to various local buyers. So completely had the station been stripped that at first Sir Frederick and his party feared that Whitey might have sold even its small staff into slavery or to some visiting Indians from the interior, looking for new raw material for dried heads.

The discovery of Whitey Dahl's exceptional merchandising ability marked the abrupt end of his career in Ferry Command, but he later went on to other activities in postwar civilian flying. These occupied his special talents until his death in 1956, in the crash of a DC-3, while flying a load of Dew Line freight between Chimo, Quebec, and Frobisher Bay.

There were a few other Ferry Command pilots, of course, who also tried to turn a little profit while flying military aircraft to various points in the world where customs inspections of such arriving planes were fairly casual. Sometimes the smuggling was carried out in the innocent interests of romance and sometimes in pursuit of vulgar monetary rewards. The constant stream of ladies' silk and nylon hosiery across the Atlantic from Canada was so brisk that the Montreal manufacturers of such items were hoping the war would never end.

"The homeliest pilot who ever flew an airplane became a veritable Clark Gable the moment he arrived overseas with a couple of dozen pairs of silk stockings," observed one member of the Atlantic-hopping fraternity.

Someone discovered that an acute wartime shortage in some foreign lands made false teeth an extremely valuable commodity. Those who responded to the laws of supply and demand didn't try to smuggle the whole upper and lower plates, just the loose teeth which could be easily carried in by the pocketful.

Occasionally, an ambitious entrepreneur tried to really break into the big time while flitting hither and yon about the globe. One night, strolling down the street of a North African city and trying to look nonchalant as he carried a travelling bag heavily laden with gold bars, a pilot was picked up by the military police. What made the whole incident particularly humiliating for him was that he never would have been bothered at all by the MP's had he not been violating the curfew rules, which were then quite strict in some North African localities.

Chapter Seven

M ost of the new hands coming in to fly for Ferry Command were lodged in the Mount Royal Hotel until they could find more permanent accommodation in Montreal or Dorval. Considering that the ferrying operations were a serious wartime activity involving the safe movement of military aircraft to the battle zones across the Atlantic, it would seem only reasonable to assume that such matters as written orders concerning the movements of crews and aircraft would be surrounded with a great deal of cloak-and-dagger secrecy. But, strange as it might seem, such orders often were posted quite openly upon a bulletin board in a kind of casually frequented pilots' common room of the Mount Royal. An enemy agent could have passed in and out with virtual impunity. Even so, there doesn't appear to have been a case in which any Britain-bound aircraft were lost, or even delayed as a result of enemy intelligence activities within the highly relaxed atmosphere of the Mount Royal.

The chances are, of course, that had some prowling German spy been caught snooping around Ferry Command premises, the man who would have nailed him would have been none other than Air Commodore Griffith James (Taffy) Powell, an extremely tough and sharp-eyed officer who had been piloting the big Imperial Airways flying boats across the South Atlantic before the outbreak of the war. The veteran ocean-hopper was what might be called a stout fellow, in more ways than one. He looked a bit portly, but most of it was muscle. Although Air Chief Marshal Sir Frederick Bowhill was the head of Ferry Command, much of the day to day operation of the service was in the hands of Flight Director Powell. It was a responsibility he handled with a great deal of ingenuity and gusto, as well as a certain regard for discipline, so far as it possibly could be applied to such a motley and lively crew of civilian and military individualists.

One morning, as Powell rode in his car from Montreal out to operation headquarters at Dorval, he spotted on the road ahead of him a trio of hitchhiking Ferry Command pilots who at that very moment were supposed to be at the airfield, preparing for takeoff. The horrified hitchhikers, recognizing Powell's chauffeur-driven car at about the same moment he spotted them, guiltily took to the open fields on the gallop.

Although the recalcitrant airplane jockeys were comparatively young, slim and fleet of foot, they were no match for their superior officer. Partly propelled by stark terror, they soared high over wire fences and then looked back behind them. Everytime, they saw the Air Commodore clear the same obstacle with equal energy (if not grace), and gain on them. Finally, when he had run them down, Taffy Powell accepted their panting explanation that they would have been aboard their airplane long ago had their car not broken down. What they had done had not provoked Powell's wrath as much as the insult of trying to run away from him after they did it. He was that kind of fellow, and was highly respected by a band of adventurers who did not give such respect freely.

Ferry Command eventually extended its operations to include occasional runs down to the West Indies on errands of various kinds. The crews sometimes stowed away on the return journey to Dorval as many cases of rum and other alcoholic goodies as they could carry in their aircraft without overdoing it to the point of the obvious. Liquor was then rationed in wartime Canada, in pitifully small monthly amounts. Some of the more experienced drinkers complained they often *spilled* that much before they could even get their first shot poured in the morning, particularly after a hard night in the Piccadilly Club. Ardent spirits were therefore a precious commodity indeed, and customs clearance of such flights, when they returned to Dorval, seldom presented any great problems.

On one occasion, Bill Vanderkloot and Taffy Powell flew Air Chief Marshal Sir Frederick Bowhill down to Puerto Rico, to inspect a base that Ferry Command had established on the sunny island. By the time they were ready to return to Dorval, two days later, Powell and Vanderkloot had thoroughly checked out the rum situation on the island.

Just before takeoff time they arrived at the airport with several cases of the stuff. It happened, however, that the Air Chief Marshal was holding a farewell review of the base personnel when Powell and Vanderkloot pulled up in their car near the aircraft. A reviewing stand had been set up beside the big machine, where Sir Frederick solemnly was taking the salute. Because their flight plan called for departure immediately after these ceremonies, the smugglers decided they'd better not waste any time. While the Air Chief Marshal was standing there on the platform directly in front of the doorway of the aircraft, his hand raised to cap, Powell and Vanderkloot were extremely busy right behind him, stowing the cases of rum aboard *Commando,* in full view of the R.A.F. airmen who were marching by so smartly with eyes right. But, emergency situations sometimes called for such drastic action.

Although the doughty Taffy Powell was quite capable of becoming involved in such nefarious activities himself, his smuggling subordinates were well aware that he was a dangerous man to encounter back in Dorval at the wrong time. Not that he was opposed to his men enjoying a cheering cup when they weren't flying. That would have been ridiculous. But there was always the risk that he might be planning some special social function in the mess, which suffered a chronic shortage of liquor. On such occasions, the homecoming aircrews, while stealthily removing from their airplanes the precious plunder of the Indies, were sometimes frozen in their tracks by the terrible voice of Air Commodore Powell thundering out a command to a waiting pair of military policemen.

"Those fellows are *smuggling liquor!*" he would bellow. "Confiscate six cases of it at once, men."

That the downcast smugglers might get a few drinks of their own booze at the upcoming bash helped ease their chagrin a bit, but not much.

Liquor was not the only thing that was brought back from the exotic places visited by pilots of Ferry Command while carrying out the errands which took them to so many far-off parts of the world. Bill Vanderkloot once greatly startled his family by walking into their apartment leading a huge Newfoundland dog he had just flown back from Gander. Other fliers also shattered the normal tranquility of their Montreal households by returning from afar with such exotic pets as parrots, monkeys, crocodiles and at least one young and affectionate boa constrictor.

Fortunately, the severe Canadian wartime rationing of liquor by the bottle didn't seriously curtail the amounts available by the glass and at considerable expense in Montreal's bars. This no doubt contributed greatly to the popularity of the Mount Royal's Piccadilly Club as a hangout for off-duty Ferry Command pilots, including those living with their families in presumably domestic bliss within their own Montreal households. The trouble was that some of them occasionally forgot to come home for a few days.

One evening the attractive and high-spirited French-Canadian wife of a pilot who had been A.W.O.L. from his family hearth for almost a week came into the Piccadilly Club looking for him. Assured by some of his loyal comrades that he had had to fly off on some special and mysterious official mission, she accepted their invitation to sit down for a moment and partake of a little refreshment. While daintily sipping her martini on the rocks, she accidentally let her handbag fall to the floor. When one of the gallant airmen hastily bent down to retrieve it for her, a large and extremely mean-looking pistol tumbled out of it. Gingerly replacing the pistol, her benefactor passed the handbag back to her with startled and questioning gaze.

"If I'd found that son-of-a-beetch sitting around in here with some other woman," she sweetly explained, "I was going to shoot him, right between the eyes."

The rather rude appellation she applied to her missing spouse might have been inspired by simple wifely jealousy and exasperation. On the other hand, those who knew them both were inclined to make allowance for the fact that her husband had been her tutor in learning such uncouth English words in the first place. It seems that he had met the love of his life while she was serving as an almost bilingual French-Canadian stewardess on an aircraft which he captained for a small Canadian airline. One evening, upon setting out from Montreal for New York on one of the fairly frequent winter occasions when the Canadian city was being attacked by freezing rain and sleet, he suggested that she warn the passengers concerning the slippery condition of the steps of the embarkation ramp.

"Tell them to be careful," he advised. "Those steps are a real son-of-a-bitch tonight!"

He first fully realized how much she loved and trusted him as a teacher of English when he discovered her standing beside the open door of the cabin a few minutes later, giving each startled passenger the same smiling greeting.

"Good evening," she was cheerfully saying to one and all. "Please watch those steps, they are a real son-of-a-beetch tonight!"

As mentioned earlier, the movements of aircraft and crews in and out of Dorval were surrounded by little or no security within the Mount Royal Hotel. This casual attitude, however, by no means extended to the personal movements of individual pilots who happened to be married. In this department, security was

54

so tight that when the bartenders answered telephone calls from wives, no pilot *ever* was admitted to be present in the Piccadilly Club. The system worked fairly well, except when Ada, the helpmate of Duke Schiller, happened to call. Here the evasive answer was of little avail.

If Duke Schiller *were* there, no matter how far from the telephone, his wife could easily hear him talking so clearly and distinctly that even the most cautious bartenders in the place finally gave up the folly of making obvious liars of themselves by saying he wasn't there.

In spite of the wide difference in their personalities—Schiller the loud and brash extrovert veteran of the Canadian bush flying trade and Vanderkloot the rather reserved and conscientious graduate from Culver Military Academy and a U.S. airline—the two hit it off well from the first day they became roommates at the Mount Royal Hotel. Early in their careers as pilots with Ferry Command they agreed that transocean hops were vastly different from flying over fairly well mapped masses of land and that if they were to survive and be successful on the North Atlantic ferrying runs, they would have to become proficient in celestial navigation. Out over the vastness of the ocean there were no familiar landmarks to guide you. There were only the stars to point the way.

It was their good fortune that soon after Vanderkloot and Schiller had made this prudent decision, they were taken in hand by Wing Commander Bill Wight, navigation officer for R.A.F. Ferry Command, who took great pains to teach them the rudiments of a science in which he was a recognized expert. Night after night, on the rooftop of the apartment house where Wight lived, he gave them special lessons in shooting the stars with the sextant and making use of this information by plotting various practice courses.

Bill Vanderkloot was to become so accomplished in aerial navigation that he would later receive from the British Government an Order of the British Empire for his work in setting up a complex system of navigational aids for Ferry Command crews arriving in the United Kingdom. Later, in the postwar years, he would write a highly respected U.S. text book on aerial navigation. But Duke Schiller's new-found skills could not save his life when later on, in 1943, after turning back with engine trouble incurred while ferrying a Catalina flying boat from Bermuda across the Atlantic, he crashed the aircraft in an attempted glassy water landing at night, killing all aboard.

Just before his death, Duke was to have moments of pleasure while based at Ferry Command stations in such delightful climes as those of Bermuda and the Bahamas. At a party one night in the Bahamas, Duke Schiller found himself being introduced to the Duke of Windsor, who was serving then as governor of the islands. He was, of course, presented to His Royal Highness simply as "Duke" Schiller, the nickname by which he was known to all of his comrades. The story is that the Duke of Windsor, somewhat perplexed to meet this other Duke of whom he had never heard before, kept wrinkling his brows, as though mentally riffling through the pages of *Burke*'s *Peerage* in a desperate effort to recall some mention of him. However, none of Duke's fellow pilots bothered to enlighten His Royal Highness on the matter and it is said that he continued to treat Duke Schiller throughout the whole evening with that certain extra shade of deference which one member of the nobility is more or less obliged to display toward another.

Chapter Eight

On April 25, 1941, after undergoing a series of familiarization and check flights on Hudson bombers, Bill Vanderkloot was the subject of a crisp report under the letterhead of the C.P.R. and over the signature of R. Stafford, Flying Instructor. It read as follows:

REPORT ON MR. VANDERKLOOT—CHECK FOR
COMMAND

General handling and taxiing	Good
Instrument flying and one engine landing	Good
Night landings	Very Good
Recommendations	Promotion to Captain
Remarks	Very Good Pilot

Naturally, the new recruit to Ferry Command was pleased to be the subject of such a highly favorable verdict, because sometimes a pilot couldn't be quite sure of how he was doing until the moment of truth at last arrived in the blessed, or cursed, form of such brief, typewritten tidings. Sometimes the check pilots and instructors, observing with an eagle eye the behavior of some newcomer as he wrestled a Hudson into the sky and back again, were too restrained and mysterious in their comments on his progress, or lack of it. Chief Instructor Dick Allen, tired of personally breaking the bad news upon those who didn't make it felt compelled to issue the following memo to those who were screening the new pilots from near and far. "In recent cases," it stated, "of pilots and other trainees being released as unsuitable from the Organization, a marked astonishment, whether real or assumed, has been manifested by the person concerned. In future please ensure that trainees and persons under instruction are informed verbally of your assessments with regard to their capabilities or any test they have undergone.

The instructors at the Dorval headquarters of Ferry Command had their own trials and tribulations to cope with. Some of these were rather embarrassing. On one occasion, for instance, a fresh recruit while carrying out a familiarization flight in a Hudson ran into a problem when he couldn't get his retractable landing gear down as he prepared to alight. After the pilot had been flying around aimlessly for awhile wondering what to do, an instructor took up another Hudson and flew along beside the rookie. By radioing several sets of instructions and observing the results, he finally managed to guide the worried pilot into positioning his wheels properly for landing. The instructor, flying along behind, then told him to take the Hudson in, which he did quite nicely.

With a certain amount of smug satisfaction, the instructor made his own final approach, ruminating on how flying wisdom and expertise so often paid off in hairy moments. His thoughts were rudely interrupted a few moments later, however, when a loud scream of tortured metal on the Hudson's formerly nice smooth belly reminded him that, in all of the excitement, he had forgotten to put his *own* wheels down before coming in to land in front of a large group of highly interested spectators on the Dorval tarmac.

Still, the cool and steady hand of an old pro was something to be mighty thankful for during those tense moments of sharp crisis which often arose when they were least expected.

In the winter of 1942, Captain J. S. Gerow was aloft over Montreal, test-flying a Boston bomber which had just arrived from the U.S. for delivery to Britain. With him was a technical assistant named H. Griffiths. While Griffiths was moving about the cockpit of the Boston, a floor panel suddenly became dislodged and he plummeted through the opening. Barely managing to grab hold of a lower section of the fuselage, he hung below the aircraft at arm's length in the bitter cold.

There was no way in which Gerow could go to his assistance and it was a certainty that within minutes the frigid slipstream would numb Griffiths' hands and force him to release his grasp upon the piece of cold metal which was all that held him away from certain death. Captain Gerow's reaction to this nightmarish situation was swift and sure. He headed at once for the frozen surface of nearby Lake St. Louis, glided down over it until the Boston's propeller tips were spinning only inches above the ice, and slowly circled the lake until Griffiths let go. So successful was this split second manoeuver that although Griffiths went skittering across the ice at terrific speed in a cloud of snow, he was able to get up at the end of his slide and walk ashore.

Only one woman flew in the trans-Atlantic operations of Ferry Command and for only one flight, but it was an event surrounded by a great deal of hot and heavy controversy that threatened for a time to disrupt the whole organization. It was a sensational enough incident when it happened away back in 1941. Today it probably would provide a *cause célèbre* for the Women's Liberation Movement. The central figure in this hectic affair was a famed U.S. woman pilot named Jacqueline Cochran.

General H.H. Arnold, Chief of the U.S. Air Force, had suggested to Miss Cochran that it might greatly dramatize the need for more pilots and aircraft for hard-pressed Britain if *she* were to fly a bomber across the Atlantic for Ferry Command. This she agreed to do and arrangements were set in motion under extremely high official auspices, which were said to include Lord Beaverbrook himself.

"The top side was thus in hand," Miss Cochran

later rather bitterly recalled in her book *The Stars at Noon,* "but no one knows better than I do that to get along it is not sufficient to have the top echelon with you. The fellow down the ranks can make or break the outsider trying to get in. That meant, in this case, the Chief Pilot and the administrators (of Ferry Command) in Montreal."

Before leaving for Montreal, Miss Cochran took what were later described as "exhaustive tests" with Northeast Airlines, and afterward underwent three days of familiarization and checkflights at Dorval with instructors of Ferry Command. According to reports, she was authorized by the "top brass" to deliver a Hudson across the Atlantic.

It was then that a rather startling turn of events took place. The Ferry Command pilots held a mass meeting and threatened to go on strike if Miss Cochran were allowed to proceed to Britain in command of one of their aircraft. Miss Cochran, describing the objectors as a "diverse set of people ranging from well trained fliers, serving for patriotic purposes, to ham and homespun pilots who were in the big money for the first time" darkly suggested that the truth of the matter was that they were after more pay; they thought the entry to their ranks of an unpaid female amateur would interfere.

The pilots maintained that she was simply not sufficiently qualified on such heavy aircraft to warrant jeopardizing the safety of the Ferry Command aircrew which would have to make the trip with her in charge—and to hell with the beneficial propaganda which might accrue from the publicity that would surround the first flight in their service of a woman pilot, and a famous one at that, across the North Atlantic. The upshot of it all was that Miss Cochran—the only woman to do so—was finally permitted to deliver a bomber across the Atlantic to the British Isles, but not without the watchful presence on the flight deck of Captain G. Carlisle, a regular Ferry Command skipper, who was to be strictly in control during all takeoffs and landings. The flight was quite successful, with no hard landings but a lot of hard feelings.

A small official footnote to the incident later appeared in the minutes of the ruling committee of the ferry operation. It read, "Finally, the subject of Miss Jacqueline Cochran came up. Capt. Wilcockson reported that physically Miss Cochran had some difficulty in handling Hudson aircraft on the ground, and it was left to him to arrange that Miss Cochran be provided with an efficient crew."

Bill Vanderkloot's first opportunity to make the big hop across the North Atlantic finally arrived two months after joining Ferry Command. As a particularly thorough and careful practioner of his art, he had come to know by then every mood and quirk of Hudson bombers. He knew for instance, that no two airplanes, even of exactly the same make and model, ever behaved in exactly the same way, no matter how identical they might appear to be. Properly nursed, wheedled and bossed, and still sensed, to some extent, through the seat of the pants (despite how elaborate their instrument panels were, compared to the rather primitive aids to flight contained on the dashboards of the old Wacos and Eaglerocks), Hudsons could be flying machines of great strength and reliability. This was always a reassuring thought, considering the thousands of miles of unfriendly ocean lying between Gander and Prestwick.

After the formation flights had been given up, the North Atlantic crossing was an operation left mainly in the hands of the individual crews. Bill Vanderkloot and his crew started out with a general briefing at Dorval just before taking off on the preliminary hop from Montreal to Gander. Most of the Ferry Command crews lived in Montreal and when an overseas flight was coming up their day started dismally early.

There was a special bus service from the centre of the city that started picking up the ferry crews at the cheerless and sleepy hour of five o'clock in the morning. Briefings at the airport began at about six o'clock and usually took an hour. They covered airport conditions at Gander, any alterations in radio frequencies—as well as changes in secret code sheets and recognition lights, which were altered from day to day—and finally, most important of all, meteorological forecasts of the weather likely to be encountered along the way.

Any aircrew receiving a personal weather briefing from Patrick Duncan McTaggart-Cowan, chief forecaster for Ferry Command, counted itself particularly fortunate. Although they irreverently referred to this Canadian meteorological genius as "McFog" (just as they sometimes referred to Air Chief Marshal Sir Fredrick Bowhill, their commander, as "Beetle-Brows"), McTaggart-Cowan was one man they all held in absolute awe. His knowledge of the fickle and vicious moods of the sky over the North Atlantic seemed almost uncanny. It must be borne in mind that at this period, out there on the sea, there were no weather ships broadcasting precise meteorological conditions from hour to hour. There were, in fact, no meteorological networks whatever, as we now know them, to flash vital weather information from sea to land and to pilots in the air.

The North Atlantic and the weather conditions prevailing from day to day in the skies above it provided a rather dark and deadly mystery, full of unknown quantities. It generated in the bravest men who undertook to challenge it the kind of fears which sometimes go with facing the unknown. As one ferry pilot so frankly and graphically expressed it, "Once we were set to get underway, any delays, particularly if they stretched into several hours, became bothersome trials, indeed. The longer you sat there, the darker and deeper and wider the ocean became, the more threatening the weather began to look and finally, if you had to hang around long enough, your sporting blood had a way of gradually turning to urine."

Small wonder that McTaggart-Cowan, who spoke in measured terms and with the reassuring air of a man who knew so well the old climatic foe and how best to meet it, was well listened to. These high-spirited and irreverent men gave him all the humble attention of those who, in Biblical times, were said to have heeded the words of the prophet who had just returned from high upon the mountain, and had seen the way.

His basic system was to divide rather haughtily, the mighty North Atlantic Ocean into ten zones. Using a method called synoptic forecasting, he would take various weather conditions as they existed over Canada—on which plenty of up-to-date information was, of course, available—and then superimpose them upon the areas he projected out over the Atlantic.

Because weather patterns have a tendency to move from west to east, what was happening in Canada one day might have a decided influence upon the weather out over the Atlantic on the following day, or the next. It was, it must be admitted, a rather rough and rule-of-thumb method when compared to today's highly sophisticated science of aviation meteorology. Yet, McTaggart-Cowan injected into his forecasts a kind of art and sixth sense so accurate that, with amazing regularity, he hit the North Atlantic weather, hundreds and even thousands of miles out to sea, right on the nose. Sometimes his forecasts couldn't have been truer or more exact had he had a whole fleet of weather ships at his disposal, spread out like a comforting string of prayer beads all across the sea.

It has been generally conceded by those who flew by McTaggart-Cowan's word, that the quiet man who later became Canada's Chief Meteorologist in the postwar years was as responsible as anyone else in the entire organization for the Royal Air Force Ferry Command's spectacular success.

Armed with McTaggart-Cowan's weather briefing and the mimeographed charts and tables which accompanied it, Bill Vanderkloot and his crew of two—a copilot and a wireless operator—set out on the first and relatively simple leg of their eastbound flight from Montreal to Gander, a distance of about 900 miles. In winter, the horrendous snows which plagued the Newfoundland airport were fought by rolling down the white stuff as it fell, until it was packed hard enough to bear the weight of a bomber. This was by no means as awkward for incoming aircraft as it might sound, because in winter, the great "sheep's foot" rollers produced a remarkably smooth and firm surface. Those who operated them had a generous way of continuing a runway, whether it was actually there under the snow or not, as long as level ground remained. This made frozen and hard-packed runways that were often longer, wider and sometimes even smoother than those of summer—provided a mild spell didn't suddenly turn them into seas of deep and sticky slush which could grab a landing airplane the way the famed Tanglefoot flypaper of yesteryear trapped a housefly.

This is how one member of an incoming Hudson's crew described it:

> We were soon over the (Gander) camp, and from the air it looked quite all right, which was our big mistake of the whole trip. What looked like bare spots on the runways was actually four to six inches of slush. Down we went with the Colonel (a passenger) and myself holding down the tail, but when we hit, it was quite apparent that all was not well. Slush, snow and water came up over the cockpit in what seemed a solid mass and for a moment I was sure we would nose over. The skipper gunned her, and we stayed all down . . . . Our inner flaps had been damaged, but otherwise all was well.

In the first days of Gander's use as a final hop-off point for the long flight across the North Atlantic, outbound aircrews who weren't continuing their eastward flight on the evening of the same day they left Montreal (a delay which sometimes occurred, due to bad weather or other circumstances), were bedded down and fed in one sleeping car and one dining car parked on a narrow gauge spur line of the Newfoundland Railway Company. Sometimes weather conditions and last-minute repairs or adjustments to their aircraft delayed some of the ferry crews at Gander for a couple of days or more.

During such periods, they ate quite well although fresh vegetables, which had to be flown in from Montreal, were sometimes scarce. But the trout from the nearby lakes, which teemed with fish, was excellent, as were the moose and caribou steaks which sometimes found their way to the menu. The railway cars which provided temporary lodgings for Bill Vanderkloot and his mates were the scene of much merriment, a few fights now and then and some extremely dogged and expensive poker games particularly for the unluckier players.

After all, most of these adventurers were dedicated gamblers by nature, otherwise they wouldn't have taken on the extremely dicey job of flying aircraft across the North Atlantic in the first place. The marathon poker games were merely a kind of concentrated manifestation of that which was already second nature to most of them. Captain "Kirk" Kirkorian, for instance, played as pretty a hand of blackjack as any man among them and for almost any stakes they cared to wager. He utilized his gambler's instincts so successfully after he left Ferry Command at the end of the war that he was able to parlay the fairly modest assets of an unemployed airplane pilot into one of the biggest fortunes in the United States. His widely varied and impressive holdings included a large airline and a couple of big hotels in Las Vegas.

But in those times, when Ferry Command gradually was blazing the now familiar trails across the North Atlantic, night life during a layover in Gander Airport was not always what might be called one long round of giddy pleasure. A pilot could join a noisy poker game in one car or try to sleep in another where the snores echoed loudly from both the upper and lower berths which surrounded him. Or, he could step outside, in the stillness of a Newfoundland wilderness night, and make the rather lonely discovery that he could hear his pulse heating, if he listened hard enough.

And there was yet another alternative. If he were rugged of physique and fairly certain that he wouldn't be setting off across the wide Atlantic on the morrow, there was the section hands' "jigger." Powered by a gasoline engine, it sat on the spur line near the railway cars and could sometimes be borrowed for an excursion to the town of Grand Falls, which owed its existence to the presence there of a pulpmill, and which usually had in stock at the local hotel a liberal supply of beer. Sometimes, while setting out on one of the Grand Falls excursions, the jigger was festooned by Ferry Command air crews, held together during the entire journey by the same mysterious bonds which enable a swarm of bees to cling in one incredible lump to a single tree branch.

The crowded travelling conditions on this jigger didn't create much of a problem on the way up to Grand Falls. But, according to the reports of the hardy ones who made the complete circuit, there was a good deal of falling by the wayside on the return journey, after a long night of song and froth-blowing in the hotel beer parlour. Those who tumbled off were retrieved, after a good deal of stopping and reversing. But sometimes dawn was outlining against the eastern sky the peculiarly sharp and skinny tips of the Newfoundland spruce trees, before the heavily burdened vehicle rattled back into the spur line behind the railway cars at Gander Airport.

The manager and "unofficial mayor" of Gander was a colorful Texan named Michael Patrick Efferson, who often regaled the ferry crews passing through his rugged domain with tales of his exploits as a stunt pilot in various U.S. flying circuses during his more youthful days. He had a particularly moving yarn about the hard times of his childhood on a small farm in Texas:

"We kids never had all the toys and things the modern youngsters have to play with. We just had to make up our own games and fun, with whatever we could find around the barnyard. We were sure poor in those days. There was one game we got very good at indeed. You know how a big cow-flap gets a kind of hard crust on the top of it after it's been sitting out there baking in the sun for a few days. Well, the way we played this game was to put our hands on the hard top, flip up the soft side and toss it at the side of the barn. Now, the main idea of this game was not to see how far you could throw this bullshit, but how much of it you could make stick to the wall of the barn!"

The enthralled audiences of Michael Patrick Efferson, lounging around on the railway cars at Gander, were usually in general agreement that the "mayor" must have mastered this quaint game extremely well and, figuratively speaking, was still mighty handy at it.

Often, during the winter months, the crews of eastbound bombers awakened in the morning to find their aircraft submerged in gigantic snowdrifts hurled against them by the wild winds of a rampaging overnight blizzard. The machines had to be dug out by shovel brigades before, like so many winter-trapped geese, they could waddle out to the hard-packed runways, their engines bellowing indignantly and the slipstream from their clawing propellers sweeping the last vestiges of powdery snow from their broad metal wings. At times it seemed strange that such wings, somehow so cumbersome and clumsy and swaying on an earthbound aircraft, could become so strong and graceful and sure once they had shed the stubborn bonds of gravity and were climbing steadily upon the North Atlantic winds.

Chapter Nine

Bill Vanderkloot and his rambunctious sidekick Duke Schiller made their first trans-Atlantic flights on the same day, flying Lockheed Hudson bombers on from Gander to Prestwick. Although such initial crossings of the "big ditch" were naturally memorable occasions for all of the Ferry Command pilots, in Duke Schiller's case the event must have provided a certain extra amount of satisfaction.

In 1927, shortly after Lindbergh had made his historic first solo flight across the Atlantic, many pilots in both the United States and Canada became severely stricken with the ocean-hopping fever. For some it proved fatal. For others it caused a great deal of keen disappointment.

Duke's first attempt to cross the Atlantic, in the fall of 1927, fell into the second category. After some years of flying about the bush in Canada's far north, he had managed to obtain some backers for an attempt to fly across the Atlantic from Windsor, Ontario, to Windsor, England, in a Stinson Detroiter monoplane called, appropriately enough, the *Royal Windsor*. With him as co-pilot was Phil Wood, son of Gar Wood, the famed speedboat king for whom Duke had once worked as a race driver. Schiller and Wood arrived at Harbour Grace, Newfoundland, on September 7, 1927, just a few hours after two old bush-flying comrades of Duke's named Terry Tully and Jim Medcalf had set out to fly the Atlantic in another Stinson Detroiter called the *Sir John Carling*.

Before Schiller and Wood could take off in their own attempt to cross the ocean, word arrived that Tully and Medcalf had been lost somewhere in the Atlantic and the news so dampened the enthusiasm of the *Royal Windsor*'s backers that they withdrew their support and the flight was called off. Now, fourteen years later, as a member of Ferry Command, Duke Schiller was having another and much more promising crack at flying the Atlantic, in a far superior aircraft, with the relish of a man who was at last completing some very important unfinished business.

Although both Schiller and Vanderkloot accomplished their first crossings without any alarming incidents, one thing about those particular flights and many later ones created a deep and lasting impression on them. *Cold.* Always, in the Britain-bound Hudsons, it was cold. At certain altitudes it was uncomfortably cold even in the summer. In the winter, it was bitterly and bone-chillingly cold. Prior to some of these winter flights, the aircraft might have been standing in the sub-zero temperatures of Gander's windswept airport for many hours or even several days. During this interval, they became frost-saturated, so deeply and completely that they never seemed to warm up, all the way across the ocean to Prestwick. Even when the temperature in the cockpit did sneak a bit above freezing, this relief soon vanished every time a window had to be opened to permit a clear navigational shot at the stars. The frigid gale which swept the cockpit while the sextant was pointed out toward the heavens was enough to inflict frostbite to the face and fingers, and cause the already chilly flight deck to become so cold that a freezer chest would have seemed like a steam bath by comparison.

Some of the aircraft carried rather primitive de-icing equipment to combat the constant menace which plagued trans-Atlantic flying at that period. It was possible to fight ice in the Wright Cyclone engines of the Hudsons by feeding alcohol into the carburetors, and to reduce ice buildup on the propellers by squirting alcohol through slinger rings on the hubs.

But there was nothing to prevent the accumulation of ice on the tail surfaces and wings, except to change flight levels to altitudes where the critical conditions which caused icing did not exist. The trouble was that sometimes you had to *climb* out of the icing zone. This manoeuver presented certain vexing problems if the wings happened to pick up rapidly a load of ice while the aircraft was already heavily burdened with the large amount of fuel required for a nonstop Atlantic crossing. Today's great jets fly miles above such weather hazards with the utmost disdain. But in the early 1940s, a pilot could soar up to the very edges of outer space only in his dreams, facing as best he could the nightmares of those treacherous zones which lay at the humbler levels closer to the land and to the seas.

Later in the war, when improved bombers did manage to achieve somewhat higher ceilings in the sky, some of the ingenious flight crews of the U.S. Air Force quickly discovered that the intense cold of the higher altitudes could be effectively utilized to overcome one of the more grievous problems of a stranger's life in Great Britain. As anyone who spent any time there during the war years knows, it was almost impossible to get a real, oldtime, all-American, cold drink of any kind. The British are, for the most part, iceless drinkers. It was extremely difficult to get a cold drink in a pub or even to obtain in a military mess enough ice to really chill a glass of beer or liquor. When the longing for a cold drink became unbearable at a U.S. Air Force base, the men sometimes took drastic action. They loaded several tubs of water into the unheated bomb bay of an aircraft, took it aloft on some kind of trumped-up mission, and cruised about at a sufficiently frigid altitude until the contents of the tubs were nicely and solidly frozen. Although such methods provided enough ice to chill beer or bourbon on the rocks for a couple of days or more, the secretary of the U.S. Treasury probably would have swooned had he ever learned these civilized amenities were being obtained in such costly fashion. But when enterprising men were desperate, expense was no object.

The Hudsons flown by Schiller and Vanderkloot safely descended upon the Prestwick Airport within an hour of each other and the tired aircrews headed off to the nearby Orangefield Hotel. This hostelry served as a roosting spot for most of the weary men who climbed out of their bombers at the Scottish base upon completion of an Atlantic crossing.

Ferry Command pilots, whose duties during the war took them to the four corners of the world, all knew the Orangefield. They talked about it with various feelings of affection and shuddering recoil wherever they gathered. For most of them, the Orangefield had been their initial safe and solid haven after their first hops across the Atlantic from Gander, which, as previously mentioned, provided lodgings of extremely primitive nature. The Orangefield was certainly no Ritz or Waldorf, but it was a welcome resting place after the long night hours of sitting on a chilly flight deck.

Most of the aircrews, having arrived at Prestwick and the Orangefield Hotel, stumbled off to bed to the glorious relief of slumber that sometimes lasted for twenty-four hours in a row. This was amazing because on winter nights many of the small rooms of the Orangefield were almost as cold as the flight decks had been. When the aircrews finally climbed reluctantly out of their beds to partake of the Orangefield's bill of fare, even their ravenous appetites occasionally became somewhat dulled by the house's wartime menu. It consisted mostly of kippered herring; sausages or "bangers" which seemed to be filled with sawdust; plenty of carrots; and occasionally a pale and remarkably tasteless omelette made from dried egg powder. Such meals were quite a letdown after the comparatively sumptuous food still available back amid the bright lights of Montreal.

But the Orangefield did have certain amenities which could not be found even at the Mount Royal

Hotel. Bert the Barman, for instance, poured an extremely generous drink, considering the British wartime austerity which governed the dispensing of such pleasures. And the two young ladies who took turns at the Orangefield's front desk won the eternal gratitude of the visiting aircrews. They set up for the men a kind of repository in the hostelry for certain highly confidential documents of a personal nature—documents which might create back home far more risk to life and limb than any mere top-secret military order that happened to fall into the wrong hands. These little black books containing names and telephone numbers of friendly lasses in Britain were handed in to the Orangefield's receptionists before every departure by an aircrew from Prestwick. If they returned, the aircrews could pick up the vital and top-secret documents and head for Glasgow or London. If they didn't return—something not uncommon in that climate of constant danger—the little black books were destroyed, a duty which the obliging young ladies at the Orangefield performed with touching loyalty and diligence.

When Duke Schiller and Bill Vanderkloot learned there would be a layover of several days in Britain before accommodation could be provided for them aboard a ship that would carry them back to Canada (the east-to-west aerial flights on what was to be called the Return Ferry having not yet been established), they joyously set out on the overnight train from Glasgow to see for the first time the fabled sights of London. Having just received their baptism on the North Atlantic run of Ferry Command, they were naturally in a mood to celebrate. Debarking from the overnight train, they checked into the Strand Palace Hotel. There was an air raid the first night they were in town, and as so many Londoners did during the early stages of the war, Duke Schiller and Bill Vanderkloot stood outside during the blackout, instead of taking to the shelters. With fascination, they watched the drama taking place far up in the high, dark skies. The great searchlights swept to and fro and when the guns in Hyde Park went into action, their thunder seemed to shake the buildings of London's West End down to their very foundations. It was hard to realize, as they gazed up into the menacing night sky, that the tiny flicks and sparks which glinted far overhead were actually large anti-aircraft shells bursting with murderous fury in the vicinity of the hostile bombers which dared to invade the heavens over the proud and ancient city.

The air raids which took place during those first and later visits to London somehow reminded Bill Vanderkloot of the sudden summer thunderstorms which swept across Lake Michigan upon Lake Bluff in the days of his childhood. First came the warning siren. Then a phenomenon resembling the calm before the storm, as the footsteps on the dark streets faded away and a comparative stillness descended upon the city. Then the distant rumble, far down the Thames Estuary, as the first anti-aircraft fire growled, like the approach of violent summer lightning. Next, the crashing sounds, like those of bolts striking nearby, as the anti-aircraft batteries within the heart of the great city went into action. Finally, the full tumult of the raging storm, as nearby batteries sounded their loud "whams," mixed with the sinister-sounding "crumps!" of falling bombs. Then suddenly the storm had passed, with the thunder sounding farther and farther away as more and more distant batteries got in their licks against the high-flying foe scurrying back toward the English Channel.

Although London is confusing enough to a stranger at any time, Bill Vanderkloot found its streets to be particularly baffling in the blackout. He and Duke became lost, sometimes after having a few drinks, and sometimes while perfectly sober. Sometimes they got lost in the blackout and sometimes in broad daylight. And hardly ever, on this and later visits, did they manage to wander about London without getting turned around at least temporarily.

Down in front of Buckingham Palace on one visit, they looked up at the flagstaff on the roof and noted that the Royal Standard wasn't flying.

"I take it," remarked Bill to a nearby bobby, with a certain pride in having knowledge of such things, "that the King is not in residence at the palace today."

"That's right, guv'ner," replied the policeman, with the special sympathetic air reserved for visiting Americans. "No flag, no King!"

For a day or two after, Schiller and Vanderkloot prowled and pub-crawled more or less together, but one night Duke disappeared on a solo expedition of some kind. It was on the very next morning that the rather shy and fairly proper Vanderkloot received a telephone call from the hotel's manager.

"Are you a friend of Mr. Schiller's!" the manager wanted to know. Bill replied that he was.

"Then I want you out of my hotel immediately!" the manager demanded in icy tones.

Although Bill Vanderkloot never did learn all the reasons behind this rather startling request, it appeared that sometime during the previous evening, Duke Schiller and the management of the Strand Palace Hotel had become involved in a dispute so loud and acrimonious that it awakened half the guests. It sent the manager into such a fury that he was determined to kick out of his place not only Duke, but everyone with whom Duke was associated in any way. It didn't make much difference to Duke and Bill, because they were checking out of the Strand Palace that day to catch their ship back to Canada.

Later in the war, they and other Ferry Command crews would be whisked back to Montreal by air. More planes rolling off the North American production lines created more urgent demands for ferry crews and moved the British Air Ministry to provide return passages to Canada that were far swifter than the plodding North Atlantic convoys. The method did speed up crew turn-arounds and deliveries, but for the passengers involved it was sometimes a much more hazardous route than even the submarine-plagued Atlantic shipping lanes.

Chapter Ten

From Dorval Airport, near Montreal, to Prestwick Airport, near Glasgow, the distance is roughly 3,150 statute miles, measured along the Great Circle route, as the airplane flies. It would seem only logical to assume that the reverse route from Prestwick to Dorval, being the same distance, would comprise the same sort of trip.

But in the high pathways which lead through the skies, things are not always what they seem. The so-called heavens, particularly those above the North Atlantic, can be full of hellish deceit and deadly treachery. That beautiful tall cloud on the horizon, rearing up for thousands of feet into the dazzling blue sky, may resemble an innocent giant cream puff with an interesting swirl on its crest that looks like a fleecy anvil. It creates the type of skyscape much admired by movie cameramen and by those photographers who take arty pictures for airline ads.

But sometimes, within the cloud that looks like a downy couch for angels, rage whirlwinds capable of ripping to bits the strongest airplane ever built. More than one has flown into such a cloud instead of making a cautious detour around it, and emerged as so many shattered bits of bolts, sheet metal and human bodies.

To this day there is hardly any aerial route on which these winds are more suspect than that traversing the North Atlantic from east to west. In the crossing from Europe to North America, headwinds of various degrees of strength and viciousness almost always prevail. Even modern jetliners, whose mighty engines virtually lick their chops with delight while swiftly devouring vast distances, can be balked so severely by the prevailing winds from the west that their trans-Atlantic progress can be slowed down by hours, compared to the time involved in their west-to-east flights over the same routes.

Today, of course, such perverse winds merely provide a mild kind of nuisance, requiring a little longer wait at the air terminal for those who are gathered there to welcome home the casual global traveller. It amounts to a passing inconvenience, like a few snow-flurries in the path of a greyhound bus enroute from Detroit to Cleveland.

Yet in the days of which we speak that stubborn westerly headwind on the route from Prestwick to Gander and on to Dorval was directly or indirectly responsible for killing scores of brave and highly skilled men. These men died in slightly converted Liberator bombers while homeward-bound from Prestwick as passengers on what was called the Return Ferry. During all their losing battles, they never had the chance of personally fighting that headwind or cursing it, or measuring the progress of the grim contest from their own flight decks.

The Return Ferry Service went into operation on May 4, 1941, using seven Liberators which could carry the air crews back to Canada in a matter of hours instead of days. This operation was taken over mainly by personnel of British Overseas Airways, which by then had succeeded Imperial Airways as the national air service carrying the Union Jack across the skies of the world. The seven Liberators were still listed on the strength of Ferry Command and their movements remained to a great extent under its direction. But they were manned by B.O.A.C. crews, all neat and correct in polished shoes, jaunty caps and properly creased navy blue uniforms.

On the flights from Dorval to Prestwick, the ferry crews were still the rather mixed and nondescript but proudly individualistic aerial adventurers who relied so heavily upon their own particular kinds of skills and ingenuity to make their crossings safely. On the way back, they were merely human cargo, with no rights, privileges or responsibilities on the flight decks of the aircraft which carried them.

They were crammed into the dark bomb bays of the Liberators with a few sandwiches and some vacuum bottles of tea and coffee which may have started out hot but were invariably as cold as a polar bear's behind after the first hour or two out of Prestwick.

When the B.O.A.C. pilots flew high in an attempt to hurdle bad weather, as they often did, the gloomy bomb bays in which the returning aircrews huddled became intensely cold. It was a cruel and penetrating cold, against which even the heavy sheepskin flying suits worn by the aircrews provided little protection. They had to sit or lie in cramped positions for hours on end, carefully sharing sips of oxygen taken from tubes which were passed from one to another. The ordeal had to be suffered without even the small diversion of looking out a window to assure themselves that there was still nothing to see, except an endless expanse of ocean and sky. For those in the bomb bay, there was just a windowless wall at which to stare through the darkness.

In such bleak surroundings, many of the aircrews of Ferry Command spent the last few hours of their lives. Greenhorns on the Atlantic run may have only a few nights earlier been tossing uneasily in their beds in Montreal, dreaming about engine failures, ice-coated wings, faulty compasses and other traps which possibly awaited them along the Dorval-Prestwick run. Now they thought they had at least placed that particular trial behind them and soon would be rejoining their families in a breakfast of real fresh Canadian eggs and bacon instead of Scotland's awful wartime sausages.

Some of them had not even had time, at the eastern end of their great adventure, to pick up a couple of real souvenirs of the proud event. They had to settle instead for hastily purchasing some packs of British cigarets, while the skipper of a westbound aircraft of the Return Ferry was impatiently awaiting only a few more passengers to make up a full load. They may have taken some consolation, while huddled later in the bomb bay, in the thought that next time they'd surely make it down to glamorous London. Many of these new fliers never made it, down to London or back to Montreal or anywhere else except to a rendezvous with death upon the slope of some desolate Scottish or Newfoundland hill.

As the Liberators of the Return Ferry fought against the constant headwinds on the way back to Newfoundland and on to Montreal, they were faced by two converging and fateful lines which, if drawn out on a chart, could have had the word *Doom* spelled out in large letters at their apex. Let us say that one line represented the ferocity and height of the westerly headwinds. The other traced the ever-decreasing supplies of fuel. The nearer the aircraft approached the western shores of the Atlantic, the closer these two fateful lines drew together. If all went well, which it usually did, there was still at least a fairly comfortable space left between them as the Canada-bound aircraft entered the final leg of its approach to the Gander runway. But there was never a wide, luxurious, extravagant space.

If God and the elements suddenly turned sour—a not uncommon shift of winter mood in the bleak Newfoundland area—the space between these critical lines rapidly narrowed in frightful fashion, until it became so minute that no room whatever was left over for even very small mistakes. Unusually dense fog or heavy blizzards at the end of a long overseas struggle against unexpectedly violent headwinds left the fate of the aircraft, its crew and all of its passengers balancing upon a razor-sharp edge between salvation and disaster—the pilot praying that the dropping needles of his gas gauges did not really mean what they were so plainly and harshly saying.

On February 9, 1943, Captain G.P.M. (Pat) Eves, one of B.O.A.C.'s most experienced pilots and a man

78

who had flown Imperial Airways flying boats on the distant Empire routes in the days before the war, sat narrowly watching such a set of dials as he approached the coast of Newfoundland. He had battled extremely powerful headwinds every mile of the way from Prestwick. The needles on the gas gauges were bouncing against the scarlet empty marks, the westerly gales aloft having greedily sapped the Liberator's fuel tanks during the sixteen-hour run.

Now the ordeal would soon be over. Gander Airport was only minutes away. The four big Pratt and Whitney Twin Wasp R-1830 engines had smoothed out again, after a few suspicious coughs from Number Three. But down below, the rugged Newfoundland wilderness was being enveloped in one of the sudden and violent blizzards so prevalent in that area at that time of year. The twenty-one men aboard the Liberator, including five members of its own crew and sixteen Ferry Command crewmen returning from delivery flights to Great Britain, began stirring their cramped limbs expectantly as Eves throttled back the Wasps and descended for his final approach to Gander. Number Two engine barked loudly in a backfire, but there was still a dribble of gas left, and all things being equal the tanks could drain completely. The Liberator was so close that it could still probably be glided into a dead stick landing on the Gander runway.

But all things weren't equal that night. When the aircraft reached the point where Gander Airport should have been, it wasn't there. Certainly not so far as the human eye could perceive, no matter how hard it might strain through the windscreen from the flight deck of the Liberator. The airport and all the country immediately surrounding it were completely hidden from view by swirling snow. There was no radio equipment down there capable of guiding an aircraft into an instrument approach. No electronic pathway upon which to slide safely earthward until at least a hazy glimpse of a runway came into view. Just a windblown hell of white, which mockingly bounced back the feeble glow of the Liberator's landing lights, as though they were merely guttering candles pitted against a solid wall of swirling snow.

Not one handy alternate airport existed in that whole vast wilderness at that time, no calm radio voice to advise Captain Eves of the wind direction and conditions of visibility at some other reasonably located landing point. Even if there had been one twenty miles away, it would have given him scant comfort, for the stark and simple reason that the Liberator wouldn't have had sufficient remaining fuel to reach it.

There was just Gander Airport down there, somewhere, amidst the blizzard through which not even one small glint of a runway boundary light could be seen. Down on the ground, huddled in their parkas and lifting the hoods from their ears to listen intently, some of the anxious men at Gander could hear the high, lonely throb of the Liberator's engines as Eves made his third and last unsuccessful pass at the field. Then there remained only the howl of the snow-laden winds. The ground crew waited for a long time, outside those snow-covered huts by the Gander tarmac, but no more sound came from the desperately groping Liberator that had used up its last drop of fuel.

The aircraft, with all those save one who were aboard it either dead or dying, lay smashed against a wooded and rocky Newfoundland slope. By morning, only one man would still be alive. Ferry pilot King Parker, who was able to walk around, had seen one of his comrades sprawled out on the ground. When he turned him over, he had no face. Then he found two more who seemed to be alive and dragged them into the shelter of the aircraft's still intact tail cone, where they huddled together through the rest of that long cold night. In the morning both his companions were dead and so stiff and frozen that Parker had great difficulty dislodging their bodies to permit his own escape from the cramped quarters where he and the two dead men had spent the sub-zero night.

It was two days before searchers found the snow-shrouded wreckage. The same cruel blizzard which had killed them had quickly covered and almost concealed them. Yet, in all that time, they were only *three miles* away from Gander Airport. They were that close to safety, after a journey of more than 2,000 miles from Prestwick. All that deadly sea between Newfoundland and Scotland lay behind them, all that frigid water had been safely crossed, and now all but one were dead, just three comparatively insignificant miles from salvation.

That was how the east-west crossings of the North Atlantic could be. Yet sometimes disaster came in strange and baffling ways on the eastern side of the sea, before a flight had little more than begun. Within minutes of taking off from Prestwick, for instance, two Canada-bound Liberators crashed into Scottish hillsides in 1941, one on August 10 and the other on the 14th of that same tragic month, carrying forty-four men to their deaths. Most of them were returning Ferry Command aircrews, but among them was Rt. Hon. Arthur B. Purvis, P.C., a leading Canadian industrialist. As head of the British Purchasing Mission in North America, he was one of the key figures in the British war effort during the grim and arduous days when the United Kingdom was trying so desperately to re-arm against the expected German invasion.

Not that the west-to-east route always remained free of mishap and tragedy during those early and highly perilous days of trans-Atlantic aviation. In February of the same year that Arthur Purvis and his fellow victims lost their lives in Scotland, another brilliant and renowned Canadian, Sir Frederick Banting, co-discoverer of insulin, was killed in the crash of a Britain-bound bomber shortly after taking off from Gander in Newfoundland. The great scientist, whose discovery, it's said, has saved more human lives than have been lost in all the wars of mankind's history, died in the wasteful ways of great wars, in the tangled wreckage of a Hudson bomber on a snow-covered and rocky Newfoundland hill, at the very outset of an airborne mission to Britain. One of the few survivors of that crash was Captain Joseph Creighton Mackey, 31, of the Ferry Command, who was the pilot of the aircraft. But Captain Mackey's number also would come up only six months later when he died while returning to Canada as a passenger in the same aircraft that carried Arthur Purvis to his death. These were the cruel and unpredictable pranks of fate that occurred so frequently in those pioneer days of flying the North Atlantic. The trails were being blazed then for the swift high routes now followed so regularly and almost casually by the Boeing 747's and similar aerial liners, while their cabin crews purvey to their bored passengers the latest technicolor movies and champagnes of only the most superior and fashionable vintage.

Chapter Eleven

Within a year of his joining R.A.F. Ferry Command, Bill Vanderkloot's reputation as an exceptionally cool and capable pilot and superbly competent aerial navigator had been firmly established, so much so that he frequently served as an instructor to recruits who were still being taken into the service. Although the new hands all had to be qualified pilots before being accepted by Ferry Command, most of them required a few hours of extra instruction in order to gain at least a nodding acquaintance with the types of aircraft they would be delivering across the Atlantic. In some cases this familiarization period involved only about three hours of flying time before the men set out for Prestwick on the hazardous aerial journey of more than 3,000 miles.

Vanderkloot also drew some other important assignments having to do with the extension and improvement of the Ferry Command's trans-Atlantic delivery system. On one of them he went to Scotland to help set up a series of alternate landing fields which were sorely needed when Prestwick was closed in by unfavorable weather. His task was to provide navigational range plates and establish the radio facilities necessary to help the incoming ferrying crews find emergency havens when fogs and misty rains hampered visibility over the northern parts of the British Isles and put the main Prestwick base temporarily out of business.

When the desert war in North Africa increased the demand for light and medium bombers and made it necessary to step up aircraft deliveries to that theatre of battle, a South Atlantic route was established. Although it didn't present the weather problems encountered on the North Atlantic runs, it did constitute an extremely long and wearisome haul for the Ferry Command crews. Captain Vanderkloot carried out some of the original surveys which preceded the setting up of this southern route, and made several trips from Dorval down through the West Indies and South America.

The 10,000 mile journey to Cairo from Miami (which was the main North American assembly point for bombers being delivered to Africa) ran southeast, by way of Puerto Rico, Trinidad and sometimes Para Belem, in Brazil, to Natal, the point in that vast country that lay closest to Africa. This leg involved a trip of 3,800 miles. From Natal the aircraft made the 2,810-mile journey across the Atlantic to Accra, on the African Gold Coast, by way of Ascension Island, a tiny temporary roosting spot where the airstrip lay between rugged bluffs. Arrivals here had to be delicately timed to coincide with the first feeble light of dawn, in order to avoid the vast flocks of Wideawake birds. This species of large gull flew only at night and swarmed back to their roosting spots on the little island shortly after sunrise. When disturbed during their daylight siestas they rose squawking into the air in dense clouds of thousands and created for aircraft in flight, a menace which the ferry pilots took very seriously. Apart from the gust-breeding bluffs bordering the airstrip and the cranky attitudes of the Wideawake birds, Ascension Island made a fairly welcome landfall on the long trail across the South Atlantic to Accra.

At Accra, the crews of the Atlantic branch of the ferrying service took their rest and handed over their aircraft—mostly Baltimores, Hudsons, Marauders, Bostons, Dakotas and Mitchells—to another division of Ferry Command. Their crews then flew them on the final 3,376-mile leg across Africa to Cairo by way of

Lagos, Maiduguri, Fort Lamy, El Fasher, Wadi Seidna and Wadi Haifa. For the most part, they were old hands at flying this long and dangerous route across steaming jungles and scorching deserts. The *harmattan,* an ill and persistent wind in those regions, sometimes kicked up sandstorms which created great clouds of dust extending as high as 10,000 feet up into the African skies and severely hampering visibility.

Occasionally those involved in the Atlantic phase of the ferrying operation didn't get a chance to stretch their legs gratefully in Accra and hand their aircraft over to another aircrew. Such frustration, for instance, was encountered on one trip by George Phillips, a veteran Canadian bush pilot serving in Ferry Command as a member of the R.C.A.F. As he and his navigator, Bill Campbell, approached the African coast in a Hudson, the weather suddenly turned quite sour, with dense cloud covering the western portion of the mainland. They discovered, when they tried to obtain a radio bearing, that their wireless equipment had ceased to function.

For some time they groped their way through the heavy cloud layers, wondering how long their fuel supply would hold out before they had to go down to a blind forced landing in the depths of the trackless jungle. Their tanks were almost exhausted when a miracle occurred. A small break opened up in the cloud cover and there below them, plain as plain could be, they saw a landing strip extending through the jungle. Slipping down through the hole in the overcast sky, whispering a few fervent words of grateful prayer, Phillips went skimming across the jungle tree tops toward the end of the runway. Just before he set the Hudson's wheels down, he noticed a ladder lying across the end of the strip, and concluded, with no little annoyance, that that was one hell of a poor way to run an airport, even in the jungle. Next thing he knew, the Hudson's landing gear was being torn off like the legs of a well-cooked turkey at a tempting Christmas dinner.

In his anxiety to get the Hudson safely down on

this hospitable-looking airstrip, he had failed to notice that a number of upright steel rails had been imbedded in the runway. This was *indeed* a hell of a way to run an airport he thought, as the Hudson careened along to a stop in what had become a violent belly landing. The disappointing mystery of it all was explained when, after climbing out of their Hudson, Phillips and Campbell were greeted by several African soldiers pointing guns with muzzles which looked, at close range, like the entrance to the Holland Tunnel in New York.

They had, it turned out, made the rather grievous navigational error of landing on an airstrip at Cotonou, in Dahomey, which happened to be under the control of the Vichy French Government, who promptly placed them in the "slammer." After staying there for several months, they were liberated by the Allied forces, during a shift in the fortunes of war in that part of Africa. The steel rails had been stuck into the airstrip in an effort to thwart a feared airborne invasion of the area by the Allies. On the other side of the Atlantic, the families of Phillips and Campbell had simply received word from the R.C.A.F. that they were missing on a ferry flight across the ocean. The letters of reassurance to their families the prisoners had posted immediately after being captured did not reach them until two weeks after the airmen had been released and returned home. The pilots seemed to be coming back from the dead because, having heard nothing more about them for months, their families naturally had assumed by then that they had been lost at sea.

Scarcely less hair-raising, in its own way, was the misguided emergency landing of another pilot on the African ferry route. After developing engine trouble during a night flight over the forbidding wilderness of jungle and sand, he was immensely relieved to spot down below him what was obviously a landing strip, complete with flares burning on either side of it. Thinking grateful thoughts as he glided through the darkness, down toward the end of the strip, he suddenly made the horrible discovery, when it was too late to do much about it, that what he had taken for a flare path was actually two long lines of campfires burning in front of the huts of a native village. Miraculously, no one was seriously injured in the extremely rough landing which followed, but the astonished airman found himself in the centre of a tremendously loud and indignant community uproar when he climbed out of his severely bent aircraft.

Chapter Twelve

Captain Bill Vanderkloot's first assignment to *Commando* took place in June of 1942 when he flew Minister of National Defence J. L. Ralston, Minister of Munitions and Supply C. D. Howe, and several other Canadian government officials from Dorval to Prestwick in the converted B-24. It was the beginning of a long and exciting association with the big aircraft that would take him and his carefully selected crew to many strange and distant parts of the world. *Commando* carried passengers of such vast importance to the Allied cause that to down it on one of these vital missions would have been to the German High Command a victory at least equal to that of sinking a major Allied battleship.

This uncomfortable thought occurred to Vanderkloot many times during the lonely hours of the night, as he sat at the controls on the flight deck of *Commando,* her four 1200 h.p. Pratt & Whitney Twin Wasp engines steadily droned away, whirling her three-bladed Hamilton Standard propellers as they chewed up the many lonely miles which lay between the huge black aircraft and her destination. On the return portion of Vanderkloot's first trans-Atlantic "V.I.P." flight in *Commando,* he flew Foreign Secretary Anthony Eden out of London on a mission to Washington.

Commando had a maximum range of seventeen hours at a normal cruising speed of 225 knots, which made her one of the best aircraft then in service for the long hops required in carrying out her special and peculiar errands.

It was only a few days after arriving in Britain on a second mission that Vanderkloot was ordered to proceed in *Commando* from London to Bathurst in West Africa, carrying Lord Swinton, British resident minister in that area. As usual, *Commando*'s departure was timed to take full advantage of the darkness, which was her main protection on such flights. They planned to arrive at their destination as soon as possible after the first light in the morning.

All went well on the London to Bathurst flight until *Commando* neared the African coast just before dawn. A heavy cloud layer obscured the stars from which Vanderkloot would normally have obtained a navigational fix. They decided that radio operator Russ Holmes would seek a radio bearing from the R.A.F. station near Bathurst. Holmes worked at his telegraph key for a few minutes and then, scratching his head, turned to make a bewildered report to Captain Vanderkloot.

"I think I got the information I needed, which is all just dandy, except for one puzzling thing . . . ."

"And what's that?" asked Vanderkloot casually.

"Well . . . the damned signals are coming from a *Luftwaffe* station in Dakar! Not only that, but they don't seem to be taking any great pains to disguise the fact."

The Dakar air base was located quite close to Bathurst.

"Oho!" said Vanderkloot. "Well, we're sure as hell not going to fall for any of that jazz! We'll stay out here at sea until daylight, when we can make a visual approach without any radio help. Wouldn't the dear old Luftwaffe just love to give us a bearing that would take us right over their station and smack into their mitts!"

Flight engineers Affleck and Williams ran practised eyes across their instrument panel. There was still enough left of *Commando*'s maximum fuel load of 3,500 gallons to keep the big aircraft slowly cruising, with flaps partially extended, for several more hours. They were far enough out to sea to be beyond the effective range of any fighter from the Dakar Luftwaffe station who might make so bold as to come out looking for them in the darkness. To complete the final leg into Bathurst in full daylight also presented certain problems, considering the closeness of the Dakar station to their destination. But Vanderkloot figured that if he approached the African coast as closely as possible under cover of darkness and then made a beeline to Bathurst at the first glimmer of dawn, the chances were fairly good that he wouldn't encounter enemy opposition—provided that *Commando* maintained complete radio silence. The German fighter base must have no clue that the big aircraft was ignoring the mysterious radio fix provided by the Luftwaffe and was lingering out there over the Atlantic, instead of continuing on to Bathurst.

But, why in hell had the Dakar station tried to appear so helpful in the first place, Vanderkloot wondered? He had never heard of such a crazy thing before. Surely the Germans didn't think he would be so stupid as to accept their kind invitation to zero in, guided by their radio transmission, and obligingly ride their beam right into handy shooting range. Was it all part of some outlandish trap? Or was there an eccentric radio operator, who, having spent far too many months under the African sun, had sat at his transmitter in Dakar in the small hours of the morning playing some mad prank on the bewildered servants of the R.A.F.?

With her four big Wasps throttled back as far as possible while remaining in flight, *Commando* continued to slowly circle around and around above the Atlantic until at last there appeared over the west coast of Africa the first faint glow of the rising sun. Once the coastline was vaguely visible, Vanderkloot set up a course directly into Bathurst. Along it *Commando* scurried while her captain kept two fingers firmly crossed on her control wheel. The Liberator closed the gap between her and Bathurst without further incident and skimmed in to a smooth and welcome landing at the R.A.F. station.

With Lord Swinton at last safely delivered and on his way by car to complete the final stage of his long journey, *Commando's* crew gratefully stumbled off to bed for a few hours of rest. By noon, it was too hot to sleep. Bill Vanderkloot arose to wash up and shave before setting out to have a look at the small R.A.F. station that huddled rather forlornly in the midst of the jungle. It was, he concluded, about as woe-be-gone a flying base as he had seen for some time, even more primitive than Gander had been in its early stages. A couple of dilapidated Hurricane fighters sat out on the tarmac and it looked as though two or three more were in a hangar. But the blue ensign of the R.A.F., with the red white and blue rondel in the fly, fluttered bravely in the light breezes which occasionally disturbed the oppressive blanket of heat.

Entering the somewhat grubby officers' mess, he was greeted by the R.A.F. Wing Commander who was in charge of this proud but dismally poor outpost of His Majesty's air force. His welcome was extremely cordial. Ordering up a pre-lunch Scotch and soda for his guest, the Wing Commander asked numerous questions about the big Liberator. Aircraft of such great size were at that time quite uncommon in that part of the world. So uncommon, in fact, that one of the worries of the *Commando's* crew while operating in such an area was that if the Liberator were ever damaged severely enough to require repairs involving replacement parts, it would have been impossible to obtain them in all of Africa. For the most part, the African campaign made use of smaller aircraft such as the Dakotas, Hudsons, Mitchells and Baltimores. The Liberators were usually reserved in Britain for the big raids upon German-occupied Europe.

As they chatted at the bar, Bill Vanderkloot began to unburden his still mystified and bewildered soul of the weird incident concerning the radio fix from the Dakar Luftwaffe station.

"Would you believe it?" he asked the Wing Commander. "Those dirty rascals tried to give me a radio fix that would have brought me in almost right over the blasted base, where they could shoot me down without hardly exerting themselves. What kind of morons do they think they're dealing with, anyway? And I'm damned if I can understand yet why they didn't take any pains to conceal the source of the signals. You'd have thought that they'd surely have tried to make out they were coming from your station. The more I think of that, the more it seems to have been the biggest insult of all."

The Wing Commander listened politely and patiently to Bill Vanderkloot's declarations of outrage for some time, casually sipping his drink and shaking his head with what seemed to be great amusement at the harrowing tale of deceit and black treachery. At last he carefully lit a cigaret, eyed Vanderkloot for a couple of moments with a merry twinkle in his eye, and made a startling statement.

"You should have accepted," he said, "the courteous offer of the Dakar station."

"I should have *what*?" asked the incredulous Vanderkloot.

"You should have made better use of the Luftwaffe's thoughtful gesture. It was probably a perfectly good radio bearing that would have brought you almost dead on into our station. Their radio equipment is much superior to ours, you know. Far greater power, for one thing," said the Wing Commander.

"Now wait a minute!" exclaimed the bewildered Vanderkloot. "Why in the name of hell would the Dakar station be handing out radio fixes to someone like me? Isn't there supposed to be a certain amount of ill feeling between the Luftwaffe and the R.A.F. right now—or is it some other war I'm thinking of?"

"Well," said the Wing Commander, "perhaps what you say *does* describe the local situation quite neatly, at that. There is, as you so rightly surmise, a great deal of unseemly competition at present between the Luftwaffe and the R.A.F. in the other war that's going on

Bill Vanderkloot and his dog Rex, 1932.

Vanderkloot in the cockpit of a P-12 Boeing fighter with the U.S. Army Air Corps Reserve, 1938.

Air Marshal Sir Frederick Bowhill, Commanding Officer, R.A.F. Ferry Command. (Photo— Public Archives of Canada)

Air Commodore G. J. (Taffy) Powell, Administrative Officer, R.A.F. Ferry Command.

Captain D. C. T. Bennett, the experienced Imperial Airways pilot who led the first formation flight of Hudsons across the Atlantic.

Veteran Imperial Airways and Ferry Command Captain O. P. Jones (centre) and unidentified crew members ready for a cold North Atlantic crossing in a Liberator. (Photo—Canada Wide)

Duke Schiller and Bill Vanderkloot.

Ferry Command pilot Whitey Dahl at tea with nightclub entertainer Edith Rogers, who saved him from a Spanish firing squad.

Lockheed bombers at Dorval awaiting delivery to Britain. (Photo—Public Archives of Canada)

Liberators in the grip of a blizzard at Gander, Newfoundland. (Photo—Public Archives of Canada)

By far the greatest number of casualties in Ferry Command resulted from crashes of homeward-bound Return Ferry aircraft. This photo shows a mass military funeral in Scotland for victims of a crash near Prestwick.

Top: Air Chief Marshal Sir Charles F. A. Portal (later Viscount Portal of Hungerford) who, as head of the Royal Air Force, selected Captain Vanderkloot as Churchill's personal pilot.

Centre: *Commando*'s crew returns to Dorval from first flight with Prime Minister Churchill. Left to right: Radio Officer Russ Holmes, co-pilot Captain Jack Ruggles, Captain Vanderkloot, Flight Engineer Ron Williams and Flight Engineer John Affleck. (Photo— Canada Wide)

Bottom: *Commando* rests on the tarmac at Dorval. (Photo—Canada Wide)

Churchill watches sunrise over the Nile from co-pilot's seat in *Commando*.

The sleeping quarters aboard *Commando* were small and drafty. The prime minister occupied one bunk, his physician Sir Charles Wilson the other. *V* for victory was painted by the crew on the bulkhead.

Churchill, wearing the R.A.F. Air Commodore's uniform which he chose to call his "disguise," congratulates Captain Vanderkloot following *Commando*'s safe arrival at desert airstrip at end of first flight to Cairo. At far left is the prime minister's bodyguard from Scotland Yard and at extreme right is co-pilot Jack Ruggles.

Churchill and Harriman with Stalin at first Moscow meeting.

Commando, officially designated as *Liberator* AL504, stands in the background as Molotov, Harriman and Churchill stand for national anthems immediately after Churchill's arrival in Moscow.

Captain Vanderkloot receives the Order of the British Empire at Rideau Hall, Ottawa, from Governor-General the Earl of Athlone, November 1942, for his work in installing radio guidance systems in Scotland and his route surveys for the South Atlantic ferry.

all over the place. But right here in this neighbourhood, things are a little bit different.

"You see, both the Luftwaffe gang over in Dakar and our boys here have good reason to believe that Berlin and London have almost forgotten all about us. If there's such a thing as an absolutely poverty-stricken and under privileged damned air force station, that's us—both here and over in Dakar. They seem to be much too busily engaged at the headquarters of the R.A.F. and the Luftwaffe to pay much attention to us. You wouldn't believe it! It takes us months to get a half dozen new spanner wrenches. I tell you we've been virtually forsaken by the powers that be and left here to gather mildew out in this humid damned swamp.

"Why, if either of our stations lost a couple of aircraft in combat, we'd be almost out of business, with damned little chance of ever getting back into business, the way the supply situation stands. So . . . we've arrived at what seems to be a fairly sensible solution to the problem. We've reached a kind of gentlemen's understanding to stop shooting at each other. That kind of nonsense wouldn't do much good toward the overall war effort and might do us a hell of a lot of harm, considering the pitiful state of our respective establishments.

"Oh, we make one daily pass over each other's station, for the sake of the official reports. But no shooting. None of that nonsense . . . ."

The Wing Commander glanced at his wristwatch.

"They'll be over at three o'clock this afternoon. We return the compliment at four. Stick around, and I'll show you what I mean."

At 2:45, Bill Vanderkloot and his host strolled out to the tarmac, where several mechanics were working on a pair of Hurricane fighters. Sure enough, promptly on the stroke of three, five German Me-109s came sweeping in low from the north. Vanderkloot shuddered as he glanced at the huge and attractive target presented by *Commando*, squatting there right out in the open. The German fighters zoomed noisily across the field and climbed skyward again before circling to the north. The mechanics, working on the parked aircraft, didn't even bother to look up at the ferociously snarling Me-109s as they passed overhead.

Standing there on the tarmac observing this amazing scene, Bill Vanderkloot came to the conclusion that it was certainly a most peculiar war being waged out there in that strange corner of Africa.

Chapter Thirteen

I f the Second World War was proceeding in surprisingly genteel fashion between the R.A.F. and the Luftwaffe at Bathurst and Dakar, this certainly could not be said of the increasingly grim struggle on the roof of the vast African continent. In Libya, the British Eighth Army of General Sir Claude Auchinleck was at that moment being cruelly bruised and battered by the German General Erwin Rommel's formidable Afrika Korps.

Before he could take off from Bathurst in *Commando* for the return flight to Great Britain, Captain Vanderkloot received orders from Ferry Command to pick up at Accra an emergency cargo of 57 m.m. antitank ammunition desperately required by the hard-pressed Eighth Army. As many cases of ammunition as the big Liberator could carry were loaded aboard from a depot in the Gold Coast seaport, and *Commando* was soon on its way to a distant desert landing strip designated on the military maps simply as LG-224 and located not far from Cairo.

It was a long haul indeed for *Commando* from Accra across more than 3,000 miles of African wilderness to LG-224. The route had to by-pass the usual stops made by lighter aircraft at such points as Maiduguri and Wadi Seidna, where the landing strips were too small to accommodate machines as large as the B-24.

Once, when passing through Maiduguri in a smaller machine Bill Vanderkloot had met the witch doctor. In exchange for some candy and cigarets, the witch doctor had presented him with a most wondrous straw hat which, he guaranteed, would protect him from all manner of evils and dangers, provided it was treated with great respect and always worn while in flight. Although Vanderkloot still carried this magic chapeau on the flight deck of *Commando,* he seldom wore it or any other kind of headgear while sitting at the controls, particularly in the steamy skies of Africa.

A forced landing along the way might very well have brought about the end of *Commando* and her crew. Some of the American Ferry Command pilots crossing the tremendous expanses of desert carried with them a document provided by the U.S. authorities and bearing, in Arabic, the words, "To all Arab Peoples—Greetings and Peace be upon you. The bearer of this letter is an officer of the United States Government assisting the English Government and a friend of all Arabs. Treat him well, guard him from harm, give him food and drink, help him to return to the nearest English soldiers and you will be rewarded. Peace and the Mercy of God upon you."

There was even a sentence, spelled out phonetically, which might enable a downed pilot to manage at least a brief verbal exchange with a desert tribesman. It read, *"Hud-nee eind el Ingleez wa ta-hund mu-ka-fa,"* which, if pronounced correctly would provide, it was hoped, an Arabic version of the words, "Take me to the English and you will be rewarded." But even an encounter with hostile tribesmen would have been a fate much more fortunate than that of being forced down upon a tremendous ocean of sand at some spot far from the routes of the nomads who roamed the desert. Of cruel and empty desert there was plenty. The plight of one of those who was forced down in these foresaken wastes was grimly and pathetically described in these notes, left by a Polish sergeant-pilot named Mikolajcak, whose body was eventually found on the desert sands beside his force-landed aircraft, at a point along the North African ferrying route between Wadi Seidna and Cairo:

I doubt I shall live till the morning, I am getting weaker and weaker every minute. I have only three more gulps of water and I have such a terrible thirst, I should go somewhere, but where? I am completely lost. Goodbye, we shall meet where we all have to go one day. Please see that this little money which I have is handed to my parents. I am dying, thinking of them and of Poland. I give myself up to God. *Time 20.00 hrs., 9th May.*

Yesterday I walked for three hours toward the West, but I could go no farther. It took me five hours to return, I only just managed to do it. So long as it is cool, I can still live, but when it gets hot I do not think I shall be able to stand it. Death is very near. I tried to take off, I have still ten gallons but the accumulators are flat. I fixed down the key so that it buzzed all night. I looked for help but now help will not come. I feel I shall not last long.

Time 09.00 hours, 10th May. I waited for ten o'clock in the morning. I had a feeling at that time help would come. A dream of a man dying from starvation and thirst. Oh God, shorten my sufferings, there will be no help for me, let nobody land in the desert where there are no people, as there is no way out. Just like me, it is better to be killed. The sand storm was so thick that I could see nothing.

Time 12.00 hours, 10th May. It is terribly hot, I drink, or rather I lick, my scanty sweat. I am suffering terribly.

13.45 hours—I hear an aircraft flying to the south, to my right, my last hope, I cannot get up to have a look. My last minutes. God have mercy on me.

It was early in the morning when *Commando* arrived over the pinpoint on the map that was LG-224. As Bill Vanderkloot circled to study the air strip and prepared to make his landing approach, he could see tanks and armored cars sprinkled across the desert. Heavily burdened as she was with such extremely critical cargo, *Commando* was set down on the strip with special tender care. When she smoothly rolled to a stop, the crew opened her doors and climbed out, expecting to be greeted by the grateful fighters for whom the fresh supply of ammunition surely would be a blessing straight from heaven. But no one appeared to even say hello. The whole place seemed to be completely deserted.

Commando's puzzled crew stood there beside the big machine for a few minutes wondering what to do. Then, from around the corner of a shack on the sand appeared the wide-eyed and sunburned features of one astonished British Tommy.

"What in bloody 'ell are you blokes doing 'ere?" he wanted to know.

"We've got a load of ammunition for you that we've flown all the way from Accra and we damned well want to know what we're supposed to do with it," replied the now indignant captain of *Commando.*

"Well," said the soldier, "you'd better get that plane of yours and your ammunition to bloody 'ell out of 'ere in an awful 'urry or it and all of us will be going up in the air a lot faster than you came down. See that 'ill over there? That's where our boys are. And see those 'ills over there? That's where Rommel is. You're right in the middle of no man's land and the Germans may be 'ere to take a shot at you any time now. I'm up 'ere on a scouting mission or I wouldn't be up 'ere at all."

Being quite aware of what would happen to *Commando* if one cannon shell or even a single machine gun bullet should hit her large fuselage while she was standing there laden with ammunition, Vanderkloot and his crew lost no time in scrambling back into the aircraft and gunning her motors for takeoff.

"Hand me my witch doctor's hat!" yelled Bill Vanderkloot to co-pilot Jack Ruggles as he raced *Commando* down the desert air strip, all motors bellowing at full throttle, and zoomed the Liberator as steeply up into the sky as her heavy burden would permit. It had been a nasty surprise, to fly so many miles to a destination that was supposed to be all snug and secure, only to discover on arrival there that it was nearly in enemy hands.

That, they learned, was one of the more confusing things about the war in the desert. It moved around a lot, and very quickly. So fast, in fact, that LG-224, which had been a perfectly valid destination only yesterday, was no longer one on the day that followed. Such rapid fluctuations in the ebb and flow of the desert campaigns could be particularly baffling to an aircrew, hopping hither and yon between various widely separated places in different parts of the world, carrying out transport chores.

On one other occasion, for instance, during the later stages of the desert war, *Commando* came skimming into a landing on a supposedly secure airstrip near Asmara, in Eritrea. Her crew was struck with utter horror when they opened the door of the big Liberator, and met a reception committee made up of a fully-armed Italian colonel and a sergeant.

"My God," thought Vanderkloot, "we've somehow blundered right into the hands of the Italians!"

Courteously escorted by the colonel and surrounded by scores of other Italian soldiers, most of them armed with quite impressive pistols in their holsters, they walked in a kind of numb daze to the operations shack. The next shock came when *Commando*'s crew entered the building and found sitting behind a desk a rather bored British Army sergeant.

"*What in hell* is the *deal* here, anyway?" asked the now completely befuddled Vanderkloot, when the sergeant rose to greet him.

"You mean about all those Italian soldiers?" said the sergeant, with a grin. "Well, I guess it does look a bit peculiar, to a stranger, at first. You see, not long ago a whole swarm of these blokes surrendered to a fairly small unit of our boys—seemed to be eager and happy to do it, in fact. After the surrender was done, all legal and proper as it were, the commandant of these fellows explained to our C.O. that in the ancient days of yore, the Roman soldiers sometimes let their prisoners keep their sidearms so as not to lose face, in a manner of speaking, sir. He asked whether the same kind of thing could be arranged for his men, if he solemnly promised and guaranteed that they wouldn't give us any trouble. Well, we let them keep their ruddy pistols and it's worked out perfectly fine, without an unpleasant time of any kind."

Following the decidedly hasty departure from LG-224, *Commando* flew on to Cairo, there to finally rid itself of its touchy and increasingly bothersome cargo of ammunition.

This first visit to the Egyptian capital was to be one of many for *Commando* and her crew. The airmen were fascinated by the sights and sounds of a city that fully expected to be under siege by the army of General Erwin Rommel before long. Rommel's highly mechanized forces had been slashing across the desert in a swift and almost unbroken procession of victories. The rumors around Cairo were that the confident "Desert Fox" had already selected the suite he would occupy in the famed Shepheard's Hotel when he made his imminent and triumphant entry into the Egyptian capital.

Cairo's streets were seething with troops. Arab hawkers, one for almost every soldier, peddled everything from "sisters who are all pink like Queen Victoria" to ivory elephants at bargain prices. Various purloined small military equipment could be picked up almost for a song if the vocalist were able to sweeten up the chorus with a couple of packs of American cigarets.

In this noisy and exciting place, Bill Vanderkloot and his crew considered themselves particularly lucky when they were able to get rooms in Shepheard's. But, before his first night was over in the highly touted hostelry, Bill Vanderkloot found himself hoping that if Rommel *did* lead his desert army into Cairo some day, he would also be billeted at Shepheard's. He figured it would serve him right.

Bill Vanderkloot's room was swarming with so many bed bugs that by three o'clock in the morning he gave up the battle against them and decided to move out of the place. An R.A.F. medical dispensary was located not far away and it was to there that Vanderkloot fled, prevailing upon the night attendants to fumigate his belongings and to allow him to linger for as long as possible under the showers. In all the tales he had heard or read about the legendary Shepheard's Hotel, he could not recall any mention of the ferocious unregistered guests who had put him to such shameful flight in the middle of the night.

Next day he managed to get lodgings on the fine houseboat *Egypt*, which was anchored on the Nile and occupied by the R.A.F. The *Egypt* had been used as an excursion boat for trips on the Nile during the prewar days and contained quite impressive dining rooms and salons as well as a number of comfortable staterooms. It made a convenient and pleasant haven from the heat, filth and clamor of Cairo's crowded streets. It sometimes seemed to Bill Vanderkloot that there were at least a million flies for every person in Cairo. He was glad to bid it farewell, after he received orders to return once more to Britain.

But he would be back again, before long.

Chapter Fourteen

A few minutes after midnight, on Sunday, August 3, 1942, a limousine arrived at Lyneham Airport, not far from Bristol. As it pulled up beside *Commando* looming large in the darkness, the car bearing Prime Minister Winston Churchill was escorted, fore and aft, by several other vehicles carrying a heavy security detail from the Secret Service and Scotland Yard. The skies were overcast, and from the low-hanging clouds came a sprinkling of misty rain. It was, Bill Vanderkloot had judged, a suitably foul night to slip southward over Britain under the cover of darkness, bound for Cairo with a cargo so precious that the Luftwaffe gladly would have sacrificed a dozen squadrons, or even several score, to shoot the *Commando* down.

After a few minutes of discussion between the prime minister and his party, Churchill climbed the ladder to *Commando's* cabin, accompanied by Sir Alexander Cadogan, Undersecretary of State; Sir Charles Wilson; Commander C. R. Thompson, Churchill's aide de camp; his attentive valet, Sawyers, two secretaries and one bodyguard from Scotland Yard. The prime minister was wearing one of his favorite travelling costumes, a dark-colored garment resembling a mechanic's overalls, which he variously referred to as his "zip suit" or "siren suit."

While Churchill's party prepared to settle down for the long flight through the night to Gibraltar, *Commando's* four big Wasp engines coughed a bit and then came to life, one at a time. Tiny rivulets of rain spread like liquid spider webs across the windshield on the flight deck as *Commando*'s crew ran up the engines. They observed closely the dashboard tachometers as the great three-bladed propellers clawed at the air and the bomber strained against its brakes and wheel chocks. The shudders which ran through the fuselage as throttles were advanced were those of a big black beast of an aircraft that seemed eager to be aloft and on her way. It always brought a certain thrill of satisfaction to her skipper, as he sat there in the left hand seat, making his final cockpit checks of the myriad switches and instruments spread out before and above him on *Commando*'s flight deck. *Power!* The sound of it had always had a certain melody of its own to the ears of Bill Vanderkloot, right back to those days at Sky Harbor when the Eaglerock biplanes flattened the grass behind them as they rolled away on their takeoff runs. It was the kind of music in which the practised and sensitive ear could detect the slightest false note, even more rapidly and unerringly then a symphony conductor could spot a minute instrumental falter in the orchestra.

With her crew at last assured that all was as it should be, *Commando* moved down the runway at Lyneham, slowly at first, then with a rapidly increasing surge of speed. She began her skyward climb with a sharp "clunk" of her folding landing gear. It was lifted moments after becoming airborne, in order to reduce as soon as possible any extra drag during the uphill haul through the damp mists hanging that night over blacked-out England.

Only the soft glow of her instrument panel lights relieved the gloom enveloping *Commando*'s flight deck as she winged southward through the night toward Land's End and the open sea. Vanderkloot and Ruggles peered hard from time to time down through the darkness, on a sharp lookout for the prearranged signals designed to give warning of enemy air activity in the area through which they must pass. As they winged at low level toward the sea, they spotted that night upon the murky landscape below, three faint flashes of yellow and one red (for close danger), but not one single comforting glimmer of green, all the way to the coast.

Sitting there at *Commando*'s controls, Bill Vanderkloot found himself pondering the strange antics of fate which had made him, a 26-year-old American, responsible at that particular moment and under those hazardous conditions, for the safety of perhaps the most important single figure in the entire Allied war effort. As co-pilot Jack Ruggles so wryly and somewhat irreverently expressed it, "This fellow is *England,* and if we ever dunk *him* in the drink. . . ."

"It was a mighty peculiar feeling," Vanderkloot later recalled of that first night in the air with Winston Churchill. "There was the prime minister sitting in the cabin, after being escorted every foot of the way from 10 Downing Street to the airport under a fairly massive curtain of security . . . . Yet, the moment he climbed into *Commando* and the door slammed shut behind him, all those guards just got back into their cars and went home! All the might of Great Britain was now far down there on the ground, with no one any longer really able to lift a finger to help us. I decided, after a while, to try not to even think about it, any more than I had to."

As for the prime minister, he was evidently settling down for the night fairly comfortably and with few misgivings, if any, concerning this new high adventure. In *The Hinge of Fate,* he described his departure for Cairo as follows:

> This was a very different kind of travel from the comforts of the Boeing flying boats. The bomber was at this time unheated, and razor-edged draughts cut in through many chinks. There were no beds, but two shelves in the after cabin enabled me and Sir Charles Wilson, my doctor, to lie down. There were plenty of blankets for all. We flew low over the South of England in order to be recognized by our batteries, who had been warned but who were also under Alert conditions.

During this early phase of the flight the prime

minister indulged in what was to become one of his favorite diversions on this and later long journeys in *Commando*. He came up to the cockpit to sit in the co-pilot's seat beside Captain Vanderkloot. In his younger days, he had done a little flying himself as a pilot, and did not display any great modesty about this early experience whenever he had a chance to sit behind the controls. Although Bill Vanderkloot was pleased and honored by the presence of his famous passenger on the flight deck, it didn't contribute to his peace of mind when Churchill, contentedly puffing away on his great cigar, turned to Vanderkloot with a sardonic grin on his strangely round, pink countenance, and remarked, "You know what Hitler would do to me if ever he got his hands on me, don't you Vanderkloot?"

Bill allowed that he had a fairly clear idea.

"But you're not going to let him do it, are you Captain?" said Churchill, with a twinkle in his eye.

This immediately plunged Bill Vanderkloot's mind once more upon the dismally anxious track he had tried so hard to desert, soon after taking off from Lyneham.

"As we got out to sea," Churchill later recorded, "I left the cockpit and retired to rest, fortified by a good sleeping cachet."

This "sleeping cachet" was probably administered by Sir Charles Wilson. On the other hand, it might well have been prepared by Sawyers, the prime minister's attentive valet, who, even within the dimly-lit confines of *Commando's* cabin, could always be relied upon to pour a brandy and soda of the precise height and strength to suit the highly educated taste of his discerning master. When the prime minister decided to indulge in such milder beverages as tea, Sawyers heated it up on the small propane stove carried aboard *Commando*. He always made enough extra to provide a welcome spot of "char" for the aircrew.

After Sawyers had made a few visits to their flight deck with piping hot tea, the crew of *Commando* decided they were going to like the prime minister's gentleman's gentleman a lot. The wry little man, with a dry, English brand of humor, seemed to take to flying quite well, even under such uneasy circumstances as those which now surrounded *Commando*'s furtive voyage through the dark and menacing wartime skies. He displayed toward the prime minister what the crew judged to be just the right mixture of faithfulness and devotion, combined with a certain self-confidence which protected him from any fluster in dealing with the many and sometimes mercurial moods of his illustrious master.

On one occasion, it's said, Sawyers was coping with a Churchill who was in a particularly bad mood. For one thing, the prime minister had been losing things all morning.

"Sawyers, Sawyers, where are my glasses?" he demanded petulantly.

"There, sir," said Sawyers, leaning over Churchill's shoulder as he sat, and tapping his pocket.

Getting ready for his afternoon nap, the prime minister found himself balked by another problem.

"Sawyers, where is my hot water bottle?" he asked.

"You are sitting on it, sir," said the unruffled Sawyers. "Not a very good idea," he added.

"It's not an *idea*, it's a *coincidence*," triumphantly replied the recognized master of the King's English, so pleased with his brilliant correction that he forgot all about his other troubles.

Meals aboard *Commando* consisted of quite plain fare, mostly box lunches packed in England before departure. The aircraft's quite austere living facilities didn't permit the preparation of much hot food while aloft.

Commando's cabin was fitted with two fairly comfortable rear berths and eight seats. Even though the berths might have been soft enough to lull the travellers into slumber, the chill drafts which somehow always managed to sneak through the pitch black hide of *Commando* did cause, from time to time, the prime minister to toss about a bit.

"Two mattresses had been dumped in the after-cabin, and I passed the night in comfort," wrote Sir

Charles Wilson in his diary. "The P.M. was less happy; he dislikes draughts—and after all it is rather a feckless way of sending him over the world when he is approaching his seventieth year. However, he soon forgot his discomforts in sound sleep, and when we got to Gibraltar this morning he was ready for anything."

It was after this initial journey in *Commando* that Commander Thompson sent the following note to her skipper:

> Dear Van,
>
> The P.M. has asked me to write you to say will you make sure that the windproofing of the aircraft around the beds is completed before your next trip.
>
> He suggests that the way you have fixed the blankets is all right as far as it goes, but that similar protection should be fixed round the head ends of the beds as well as up to the roof. He also suggests that some kind of windproof fabric might be better than blankets.

Commando's air conditioning was indeed a little too adequate even for an inveterate cigar-smoker.

During his evening visits to the flight deck on the way to Cairo, Churchill sometimes wore, in addition to his dressing gown and slippers, a quite spectacular multi-colored nightcap. It was perhaps the only piece of his famed and varied collection of headgear in which he had not been photographed, at one time or another. When worn with his brightly hued robe, it gave him an appearance which vaguely resembled that of some rotund and unusually fair-complexioned Oriental potentate. Occasionally, while considering the worrisome possibility of being forced down in the desert by some mechanical malfunction, Bill Vanderkloot found himself wondering, with a reflective grin, just how far the prime minister might be able to travel in his colorful night attire before the Arabs discovered he wasn't one of them.

It was during Churchill's first journey in *Commando* that the crew put up an extra piece of wall decoration on the face of the bulkhead at the back of the twin-bunk sleeping quarters. The *V* for *Victory* made a great hit with the aircraft's distinguished passenger.

The sleeping compartment also had a small cupboard between the heads of the two bunks, and an adjustable reading lamp which sat near a recess in the top of a cabinet that was large enough to contain a bottle of brandy, in case it was needed to help chase away the chills.

Housekeeping equipment aboard the converted Liberator was simple but fairly effective. The small cooking stove was situated immediately under the astro hatch, located in the top of the cabin and usually opened while making navigational shots upon the stars. But this hatch also came in quite handy while carrying out other chores. Sometimes, while in flight, the hatch would be lifted to serve as part of an ingenious kind of makeshift vacuum cleaner. By simply extending one end of a length of hose up into the slipstream, the brisk suction created at the other end could be used to tidy up *Commando's* cabin.

Living conditions aboard the converted bomber that was the pride of the Ferry Command were certainly a far cry from the luxurious airliners of today, as was its technical equipment up on the flight deck. It should be remembered that at that time there were none of the elaborate electronic navigational aids which now provide for the crews of modern airliners such familiar highways in the sky. *Commando* was merely one lonely and isolated pinpoint in the dark heavens, so out of touch with the world below that even at Downing Street or in the Air Ministry no one knew, even roughly, the whereabouts of the prime minister until he had actually landed at the completion of a flight. Sometimes, sitting up at *Commando's* controls during the long hours of the night, Bill Vanderkloot would find himself once more pondering this strange state of affairs.

"Here am I, a civilian—and an *American* civilian, at that—" he would think, "with the safety and even the very life of the prime minister of Great Britain in my sweaty hands. How could they know, for instance, whether I would take a bribe of, say, a million dollars in cold cash to fake a force landing on some hostile ground that would deliver the prime minister into the hands of the enemy?"

Later similar questions would be asked in the British House of Commons. Why was an American civilian pilot being allowed to fly not only the prime minister, but many members of the British Imperial military staff and several key ministers, when so many capable pilots of the Royal Air Force were available for this critical and demanding task? Churchill promptly replied, with his customary audacity and scorn toward such questions, that Captain Vanderkloot was flying him, members of his cabinet and some of his military leaders for the very good reason that he, the prime minister, had personally accepted him as the best man for the job. Many years later, in a conversation with this writer, Air Commodore Taffy Powell, executive head of the R.A.F. Ferry Command, agreed most emphatically with the prime minister's assessment.

"Vanderkloot was not only an excellent pilot, but also an excellent navigator and undoubtedly the right man for the job," said Powell.

Shortly after first light on the morning of August 3, 1942, Commando's co-pilot, Jack Ruggles, grinned happily and pointed ahead to a prominence boldly rearing up on the distant horizon.

"We seem to be right on," he remarked to Captain Vanderkloot. "There's that Prudential Life Insurance sign large as life, right up there, dead ahead!"

Sure enough, the great looming bulk of the Rock of Gibraltar stood out boldly against the sky. Commando's four big Wasps purred away smoothly, as they had done all through the night on the long haul from England. When they were throttled back for the approach to the rather closely cramped Gibraltar airstrip, Commando's distinguished passenger appeared in his "zip suit," gazed for a moment at the impressive scene ahead, then smiled with much satisfaction before returning to the cabin.

Gibraltar's airstrip could be tricky at times for such comparatively large aircraft as Commando, with her all-up weight of 56,000 pounds. The single runway was situated on what was called the North Front of the big rock, and it ran in an east-west direction. Its western portion consisted of a 900-yard extension built out into a sheltered bay with fill taken from tunnelling operations in Gibraltar carried on by engineers of the Canadian Army after the outbreak of the war. These men had gained valuable experience in similar work while engaged in hard rock mining in their own country. The runway continued across a narrow neck of land lying between the bay and the open waters of the Mediterranean and had a total useable length of 1,530 yards. This was a comfortable enough margin under favorable conditions, but the great lofty face of the fortress could sometimes create awkward crosswinds, updrafts and downdrafts, when the gusts were coming from certain directions with sufficient velocity. There was also the necessity of keeping a sharp eye out for the masts of anchored capital warships while skimming low from the west across the bay to make a landing approach to the airstrip.

But on this sunny day, *Commando*'s big wheels softly caressed the hard-topped surface of the landing strip with hardly a yelp of tortured rubber. As Vanderkloot gunned her engines and headed for the tarmac, he noticed a peculiar thing some distance to his left. Although it didn't disturb him much at the time, it was to inspire pronounced feelings of discomfort during subsequent stops at Gibraltar with important passengers. It was a structure that looked not unlike some kind of aircraft control tower, but the peculiar thing was that it stood on the other side of the fence which divided the airport area from the nearby Spanish territory. This was strange, because there weren't any aircraft movements taking place on that side of the fence. What this "control tower" amounted to, he later learned, was simply an extremely handy observation platform from which German intelligence agents could follow with great ease and comfort the arrivals and departures of all air traffic in and out of Gibraltar. There was little the British authorities could do about it, because Spain was ostensibly neutral and German "visitors" had free access to the country. In fact, in nearby Tangiers in Spanish Morocco, German, Italian and Allied desert troops sometimes mingled quite freely at the bars and night clubs while spending a bit of leave in the North Africa city.

Although Prime Minister Churchill and his party were carefully debarked on the side of the big Liberator that was at least partially concealed from prying eyes across the border, and were whisked away in a closed car, the German radio announced only a few hours later that the British leader had arrived in Gibraltar. This trying situation greatly disturbed Bill Vanderkloot and his crew as they planned the next long leg of their journey.

The prime minister's party was escorted from the airport by Lieutenant General Sir Frank Noel Mason-Macfarlane, Governor of Gibraltar, and Major Anthony Quayle, the movie actor, who was then the Governor's military assistant. Although a strong guard was immediately placed around the area where *Commando* was parked, her captain and crew stayed nearby during the brief stopover. They had much to do to prepare the aircraft for the next long stage of her journey. Also, it was known that agents of the Nazi *Abwehr* occasionally had managed to slip across the border between Spain and the British fortress to commit acts of sabotage on Allied merchant and naval craft in the harbor. The crew of *Commando* wanted to make certain that no such mischief should be done to the big converted bomber which was to set out that evening on the next critical leg across the vast desert area that still lay between *Commando* and Cairo.

The prime minister later described as follows the arrival and departure from Gibraltar:

We reached Gibraltar uneventfully on the morning of August 3, spent the day looking around the fortress, and started at 6 P.M. for Cairo, a hop of 2,000 miles or more, as the detours necessary to avoid hostile aircraft around the Desert battle were considerable. Vanderkloot, in order to have more petrol on hand, did not continue down the Mediterranean till darkness fell, but flew

111

straight across the Spanish zone and the Vichy quasi-hostile territory. Therefore, as we had an armed escort till nightfall of four Beaufighters we in fact openly violated the neutrality of both these regions. No one molested us in the air, and we did not come within cannon shot of any important town. All the same, I was glad when darkness cast her shroud over the harsh landscape and we could retire to such sleeping accommodation as *Commando* could offer. It would have been very tiresome to make a forced landing on neutral territory, and even descent in the desert, though preferable, would have raised problems of its own. However, all *Commando*'s four engines purred happily, and I slept sound as we sailed through the starlit night.

It was my practice on these journeys to sit in the copilot's seat before sunrise, and when I reached it on this morning of August 4, there in the pale, glimmering dawn the endless winding silver ribbon of the Nile stretched joyously before us. Often had I seen the day break on the Nile. In war and peace I had traversed by land or water almost its whole length, except the Dongola Loop, from Lake Victoria to the sea. Never had the glint of daylight on its waters been so welcome to me.

Sitting there beside Churchill on the flight deck that morning, Bill Vanderkloot was experiencing some thankful thoughts of his own. He gradually dropped off altitude, and *Commando* winged her way northward down the Nile toward the Cairo landing field. So many miles of lonely desert—some of its controlled by "quasi-hostile" governments, to use Churchill's term—now lay behind them. In some areas, the aircraft of the Luftwaffe were searching the skies above this great wasteland, quite possibly looking for *Commando*, even though she had flown at night under the comparative security of darkness. The sprawling mass of Cairo, now coming into view in the early morning light was indeed a fine sight to behold.

"Vanderkloot has brought it off," the formerly skeptical Sir Charles Wilson noted, rather grudgingly, in his diary on August 4. "We landed safely near the Pyramids and drove into Cairo."

But if *Commando*'s captain, the prime minister and most of the other passengers aboard were enjoying some welcome relaxation of their tensions, one man sitting aft in the cabin was breathing a far more fervent sigh of relief than any of the rest. He was Inspector Thomson, Churchill's bodyguard from the Scotland Yard C.I.D. All during the flight from England, in the small world of *Commando's* cabin, where a sense of "togetherness" was an absolute necessity rather than a mere social ideal, he had somehow managed to appear aloof and alone with his thoughts. And perhaps for a very good reason had he sat there so often in brooding silence.

Although his basic responsibility was, of course, to guard Winston Churchill's safety at all times, it was whispered that the orders he had received in London charged him with a much grimmer task—to shoot the prime minister should *Commando* ever be forced down upon territory where his capture by the enemy appeared certain.

Chapter Fifteen

U pon the prime ministers arrival in Cairo at the end of a successful aerial journey which had ·taken him and *Commando* more than once into the rather uncomfortable proximity of the roving aircraft of the Luftwaffe—both over England and over stretches of the North African desert where German fighters were known to be hunting in the skies, he was driven to the British Embassy, where he was to reside during his stay in the Egyptian capital. Awaiting him there was his old friend and confidant, Field Marshal Jan Christiaan Smuts, prime minister of South Africa. Determined to tackle the rather unpleasant job of shaking up and reorganizing the entire High Command in the Middle East, Churchill had requested that Smuts, one of the most respected of all the Commonwealth's elder statesmen, come to Cairo from South Africa to give him the benefit of his counsel while making the difficult decisions which now confronted him.

One of the most important conclusions arising from Churchill's discussions with Smuts and others, was that General William "Strafer" Gott should be placed in charge of the Eighth Army, under General Harold Alexander as Commander-in-Chief of an area the prime minister now chose to designate as the Near East. General Gott was a soldier whom the prime minister held in particularly high esteem, but his move to the command of the Eighth Army was not to be. While

Churchill was there in Egypt in the very act of preparing for this change, General Gott was killed. The airplane in which he was being flown into Cairo was shot down by a prowling fighter aircraft of the Luftwaffe "in almost the very air spaces through which I now flew," as Churchill later described it.

"I certainly felt grief and impoverishment at the loss of this splendid soldier, to whom I had resolved to confide the most direct fighting task in the impending battle," Churchill wrote. "All my plans were dislocated."

This tragedy resulted in the appointment of General Bernard Montgomery to command the Eighth Army; and grimly underlined the dangers which also confronted the prime minister himself, as he flew in and out of the area of the desert battle with, perhaps, the full knowledge of German intelligence. Certainly the news of the shooting down of General Gott's aircraft did little to ease the tension of *Commando*'s crew as they made the big bird ready for the next leg of its lengthy mission with Churchill.

Not until several days after arriving in Cairo was *Commando*'s captain given confirmation of what this next stage of the journey would be. Churchill had accepted from Premier Stalin an invitation to continue on from Cairo to Moscow, for a first meeting between the two leaders. Once again *Commando*'s skipper found himself faced with the heavy responsibility of planning and "pre-flying" in his mind, so far as possible, a long and potentially dangerous journey, most of it over territory with which he was completely unfamiliar and about which he had little useful aeronautical information. Even under normal conditions, in those days, such a flight would have presented certain problems. But when the importance of *Commando*'s present passenger was taken into account, the worrisome aspects of such a journey took on far greater dimensions.

By the time *Commando* was ready to depart for Moscow, on August 10, 1942, the big Liberator had acquired a new passenger, special U.S. envoy W. Averell Harriman, who at the prime minister's request, had joined Churchill at Cairo to accompany him on this momentous visit to Russia as the personal representative of President Roosevelt.

As usual, *Commando* took off from Cairo at night. Also as usual, the prime minister was in the co-pilot's seat bright and early next morning to admire the scenery and give what flying advice he considered necessary to the captian. On such occasions it seemed to *Commando*'s crew that Churchill gained nearly as much pride and satisfaction from sitting in the right hand seat on the flight deck, contributing his flying knowledge to the safe voyage of *Commando,* as he did while occupying his lofty seat in the House of Commons contributing his vast political knowledge to the task of guiding the British ship of state through its perilous journey.

Commando's flight plan took the aircraft northeast from Cairo across Jordan and Iraq to Tehran. From here, after a one-day stop, it would continue almost due north along the length of the Caspian Sea toward Kuibyshev, from which point it would follow a northeasterly course into Moscow. Churchill later described that first sunrise after takeoff from Cairo:

By dawn we were approaching the mountains of Kurdistan. The weather was good and Vanderkloot in high spirits. As we drew near to the serrated uplands I asked him at what height he intended to fly them. He said nine thousand would do. However, looking at the map I found several peaks of eleven and twelve thousand feet, and there seemed one big one of eighteen or twenty thousand, though that was farther off. So long as you are not suddenly encompassed by clouds, you can wind your way through mountains with safety. Still, I asked for twelve thousand feet, and we began sucking our oxygen tubes. As we descended about 8:30 A.M. on the Tehran airfield and were already close to the ground I noticed the altimeter registered four thousand five hundred feet, and ignorantly remarked, "You had better get that adjusted before we take off again." But Vanderkloot said, "The Tehran airfield is over four thousand feet above sea level."

Like so many other helpful amateur pilots have

discovered before him and since, Churchill had found a little knowledge could be at least an embarrassing if not dangerous thing when dealing with the professionals, and in characteristic fashion he was big enough to confess it all to history.

Churchill's request that *Commando* be taken up to 12,000 feet certainly didn't please his physician, Sir Charles Wilson, who had asked Vanderkloot to remain below 10,000 feet as much as possible in the interest of the prime minister's health. After all, such long flights in those days could be exhausting even for much younger men and at comparatively low altitudes. Sir Charles considered that to expose a man of sixty-eight to the rarified atmosphere lying above 10,000 feet on such an extended and fatiguing aerial journey might be medically indiscreet, even for a person of such seemingly boundless energy as Winston Churchill.

One of the secrets of the apparent stamina which often allowed the prime minister to be up and about at all hours of the night without any apparent ill effects was his ability to take short naps almost anywhere and at any time. Churchill had great faith in this method of conserving energy for the occasions when it was most required, and constantly preached its virtues to his military staff and other associates. One high ranking admiral was said to have been so impressed by this advice that he took to dozing during important strategy conferences in the War Room in London. Churchill later remarked that he was relieved to observe during such meetings that his disciple always snapped back into full and alert wakefulness whenever a naval subject arose.

Although Churchill didn't make many visits to *Commando*'s flight deck during the periods of darkness, Captain Vanderkloot did occasionally find him up and about at some unlikely late hour of the night when he dropped back into the passenger cabin to see if all were well. Sometimes the prime minister would be lying in his bunk writing notes or going through his papers. If there actually is such a thing as a "night person" Churchill was probably one of them.

Vanderkloot was once told by a group captain

commanding an R.A.F. bomber base in the south of England how he had had an embarrassing telephone conversation with the prime minister at three o'clock in the morning. His aircraft had set out that night on a distant and critical raid over Europe and he was sitting in the operations room anxiously awaiting news from them about how the sortie had gone. Such information could not be provided, of course, until the aircraft had proceeded far enough on their homeward journey to break radio silence. As he sat there sweating it out in the small hours of that tense morning, the telephone rang and he picked it up to find the prime minister at the other end of the line.

"What success did your men have tonight?" inquired Churchill.

"Well . . . I . . . I really don't know yet, sir," replied the startled group captain.

"Did they have any great opposition over the target?" Churchill wanted to know.

"I really don't know, sir," truthfully replied the group captain, who was having certain frustrations of his own about acquiring such knowledge.

"How were our losses, heavy or light?" asked the prime minister.

"I . . . I'm afraid I don't know," said the officer.

The response was a long and exasperated sigh from the War Room at Whitehall.

"Well, my man," Churchill finally replied. "If ever you *should know* anything, do not hesitate to call me."

Then, just before the telephone clicked down at the other end, the chagrined group captain heard Churchill remark to someone in a clearly audible stage whisper, "I don't imagine I shall be bothered much by *that* fellow!"

At the end of the first day's flying on the long trip to Moscow, the Churchill party, along with *Commando*'s crew, spent the night in the quite luxurious residence of Sir Reader Bullard, British minister in Tehran. The U.S.S.R. had at that time a sizeable military establishment in the Persian capital and from its ranks were drawn a number of extremely businesslike and formidable looking soldiers to stand guard on *Commando* while her passengers and crew took their rest in the city. Captain Vanderkloot couldn't help but feel reassured about the safety of the big Liberator as he watched the sentries taking up their posts while he and his crew drove off from the airport.

Just how conscientious the Russian guards were to be in carrying out their duties was not fully impressed upon him, however, until the following morning. With the takeoff for Moscow scheduled for 6:30 A.M., *Commando*'s crew was up and on the way to the Tehran airport well before dawn, in order to have everything aboard ready before the arrival of Churchill and his party. Reaching the tarmac where *Commando* squatted in the pre-dawn gloom, the crew hurried over to enter the aircraft and begin preparations for the flight. But they didn't get very far.

Before they could approach within 200 feet of the aircraft, they were halted by the Russian sentries. Looking with rather horrified fascination down the muzzle of a submachine gun, Vanderkloot tried to explain that he and his companions were the crew of the machine and urgently desired to go aboard to make it ready for takeoff. But *Commando*'s crew could speak no Russian and the Russian guards could speak no English, although the tilt of their machine guns spoke clearly enough. *Commando*'s crew, armed only with their English and their gestures, tried in every manner they could think of to make it clear that they *belonged* on the aircraft and simply had to go aboard if they were to have it ready by the time their distinguished passengers arrived. But the communications gap was just too wide, and seemed to grow wider and wider as the time margin grew narrower.

"For Pete's sake let's not try to force our way into the aircraft," Bill Vanderkloot muttered out of the corner of his mouth to Jack Ruggles. "I can tell by the look in their eyes that these guys will shoot us, sure as hell!"

As the stalemate continued, the time for the arrival of Churchill's party grew steadily closer. Finally in desperation, they decided to send a messenger back to the British Legation to awaken someone who could speak Russian. When a sleepy-eyed secretary at last arrived, he was able to explain the situation to the satisfaction of the captain of the guard and the crew of *Commando* was allowed to go aboard their aircraft. Not long afterward, two Russian Air Force officers arrived to accompany *Commando* on her flight to Moscow and give navigational assistance to her crew during this critical leg of the journey to Moscow. Vanderkloot was naturally happy to have them aboard and to receive the benefit of their guidance while skirting the German lines enroute to Moscow. But he found himself wishing they had arrived at the airport early enough to lead the way into his own airplane, a short enough journey but one that for a time looked even more difficult and perilous than the trip from Tehran to the Soviet capital.

As it turned out, all was in readiness aboard *Commando* by the time the prime minister's party reached the airport. She stood there looming large and black in the first light of morning while her passengers mounted the ladder to her cabin. As the ladder was pulled up and the door closed, *Commando*'s big Pratt & Whitney engines came to life one by one until the day's early stillness filled with mighty thunder and the dust of Tehran's airport rose in the whirlwinds of the slipstream. At Tehran's considerable altitude, *Commando* required a somewhat longer takeoff run than usual, but the airport was an excellent one, among the best Vanderkloot had encountered during his far-reaching missions in the big Liberator, and the plane was soon airborne with plenty of runway to spare. She had no sooner settled into her climb to cruising altitude than Churchill was up on the flight deck to occupy the seat always so briskly vacated by Jack Ruggles to make way for *Commando*'s enthusiastic unofficial co-pilot. Churchill later described the departure from Tehran:

At 6:30 next morning, Wednesday, August 12, we started, gaining height as we flew through the great valley which led to Tabriz, and then turned northward to

120

Enzeli, on the Caspian. We passed this second range of mountains at about eleven thousand feet, avoiding both clouds and peaks. Two Russian officers were now in the plane, and the Soviet Government assumed responsibility for our course and safe arrival. The snow-clad giant gleamed to the eastward. I noticed that we were flying alone, and a wireless message explained that our second plane, with the C.I.G.S., Wavell, Cadogan, and others had had to turn back over Tehran because of engine trouble. In two hours the waters of the Caspian sea shone ahead. Beneath was Enzeli. I had never seen the Caspian, but I remembered how a quarter of a century before I had, as Secretary of State for War, inherited a fleet upon it which for nearly a year ruled its pale, placid waters. We now came down to a height where oxygen was no longer needed. On the western shore, which we could dimly see, lay Baku and its oilfields. The German armies were now so near the Caspian that our course was set for Kuibyshev, keeping well away from Stalingrad and the battle area. This took us near the delta of the Volga. As far as the eye could reach, spread vast expanses of Russia, brown and flat with hardly a sign of human habitation. Here and there sharp rectineal patches of ploughed land revealed an occasional State farm. For a long way the mighty Volga gleamed in curves and stretches as it flowed between its wide, dark margins of marsh. Sometimes a road, straight as a ruler, ran from one wide horizon to the other. After an hour or so of this I clambered back along the bomb bay to the cabin and slept.

Up on the flight deck, the two Russian Air Force officers who were serving as *Commando*'s guides along this final leg into Moscow, watched curiously as the prime minister, puffing contentedly upon his huge cigar, abandoned his "flight duties" which by now were considered almost routine in the cockpit, and left to rejoin his party.

Harriman, the U.S. envoy, was not greatly impressed by the rather meager amenities *Commando* had to offer. He later wrote in his memoirs:

We went on to Tehran and from there to Moscow. I flew with Churchill in his B-24 with his American pilot. It was converted for passengers in the most primitive manner, without insulation, and with two rows of hard benches facing each other. The noise was so great it made conversation impossible. Our only communication was by passing notes to each other, some on important subjects, some trivial.

Churchill, as always, was accompanied by his naval aide, Commander Thompson, who had a delightful personality but failed at times to make all arrangements in a matter satisfactory to the prime minister. When "Tommy" produced the lunch basket, a crisis arose. The prime minister selected a ham sandwich and then demanded mustard. The basket was turned upside down, but no mustard. Churchill wrote on a note, "How could you have forgotten the mustard? No gentleman eats ham sandwiches without mustard." Tommy got back into the prime minister's good graces, however, on the return trip. This time the lunch basket was provided by the Kremlin and included caviar, champagne and other delicacies. Churchill was delighted and wrote Tommy, "All is forgiven—even the mustard."

We could not take the direct route over Baku and Stalingrad because of the closeness of the Luftwaffe on the southern front. Instead we flew well to the east over the Caspian to Kuibyshev and then on to Moscow.

Originally, it had been planned that *Commando* should make a brief stop at Kuibyshev to provide a break in the exhaustingly long flight from Tehran to Moscow, a journey that was made even more lengthy by the detours required to stay well clear of the German positions. But it was decided that *Commando* should stay aloft and continue right through to Moscow. Churchill later wrote:

The weather being clear, the wind favourable and my need to get to Moscow urgent, it was arranged to cut the corner of Kuibyshev and go on straight to the capital. I fear a splendid banquet and welcome in true Russian hospitality was thus left on one side. At about five o'clock the spires and domes of Moscow came in sight. We circled around the city by carefully prescribed courses along which all the batteries had been warned, and landed on this airfield which I was to revisit during the struggle.

Chapter Sixteen

As *Commando*, more than ten hours out of Tehran, rolled to a stop at the Moscow Airport and the ignition switches of her engines were finally cut, a large and impressive honor guard composed of hand-picked Russian soldiers goose-stepped smartly across the tarmac and snapped to attention. When the door of *Commando* opened and Churchill climbed down the extended ladder, followed by Harriman, a band struck up "God Save the King," followed by the "Star Spangled Banner" and the "Internationale." With the anthems of the three great nations played in full, Foreign Minister V. M. Molotov stepped forward to shake heartily the hands of the distinguished visitors who had travelled so far to help lay the initial foundations of the "Grand Alliance" which eventually would bring about the downfall of the Axis powers. When the arrival ceremonies had been concluded, Churchill and his aides were driven to a dacha on the outskirts of Moscow while Harriman and his party were taken into the city, to a residence where they would be lodged during the conference.

Commando's crew was taken in charge by an extremely good-natured and helpful Soviet Air Force major, who accompanied them to the National Hotel where they would reside while in Moscow. The English-speaking major turned out to be such an excellent host that he helped to alleviate somewhat the lingering annoyance of *Commando's* crew at so narrowly escaping the great embarrassment of being found under arrest by Russian guards when Churchill arrived at the Tehran airport.

However, on the day after *Commando's* landing at Moscow, an incident took place which must have dissolved completely every last shred of animosity its crew might still have felt toward the diligent Russians. Engineers Johnny Affleck and Ron Williams had particular reason to remember warmly and even affectionately what a fine bunch of chaps their Russian hosts had turned out to be.

It seems that during one of the frequent and careful inspections of *Commando,* the engineers found a tire on the big machine that was showing suspicious signs of wear. The day being quite hot, they didn't relish the prospect of wrestling to replace the big tire with a suitable new one that had been obtained from some Russian stores of lend-lease supplies provided by the United States. But the job had to be done. They had just rolled up their shirtsleeves and assembled their wrenches and other equipment when a Russian officer arrived on the scene and indicated they were to be seated in some special chairs brought with a flourish to the site of the repair job. While *Commando's* crew sat there in profound astonishment, a Russian squad took over the complete tire-changing chore! But another and even more pleasant surprise was yet to come.

A fairly large van arrived and began discharging tables which were set up in a shady spot. A group of white-jacketed and black-bow-tied Russian waiters then proceeded to adorn these tables with linen cloths, fine china that looked like it might have come from the former palace of the Czar himself, and a great array of sparkling crystal and silverware.

Next came the food—jars of choice Russian caviar, and platters of smoked sturgeon, ham and numerous other gourmet victuals. The thoroughly bedazzled crew of *Commando* was then invited to partake of this feast, in ease and comfort, while the Russian mechanics sweated over the tire changing job, under the watchful eye of a Soviet colonel. As they enjoyed the bounteous meal, Affleck and Williams agreed that the life of a visiting Canadian air engineer, there on the outskirts of Moscow, was certainly far, far superior to the kind he was forced to endure back at Dorval or Gander.

Their eager hosts not only took *Commando's* crew on tours of the Russian capital and various aircraft plants, but also on a motor trip to a point where they could sight the front being held so grimly against the invading German army. On the way, they passed through villages from which the Germans had fallen back. Here, it was said, the returning Russians had found many of their countrymen hanging by their necks from lampposts.

"We Russians," said one of their escorts, "don't hesitate to sacrifice a hundred men to stop a German tank. Would the Americans and the British do such a thing?"

Vanderkloot had to admit that although British and American soldiers were brave men indeed, there were limits to the slaughter they would endure to stop a single tank.

Back in Moscow Captain Vanderkloot and his crew were taken by their hosts to the ballet, while the distinguished passengers they had flown to Russia labored long at conferences with the Soviet leaders that usually extended far into the night. So painstaking was the hospitality of their hosts that *Commando's* crew were given special bouquets to present after the performances to the prima ballerina.

On one occasion during their stay in Moscow, however, *Commando's* crew had to admit ruefully that Russian hospitality sometimes could be carried above and beyond what might be termed the normal call of duty toward a group of visiting airmen. A party was held in one of the dining rooms of the National Hotel. It was a rigorously convivial occasion, marked by toast after toast after toast, and lasted well into the small hours of the morning. Bill Vanderkloot later vaguely recalled that at least eighty-five per cent of the guests at this hectic soiree were unable to depart completely under their own steam at the end of the affair. He believes that, perhaps due to his superior navigational abilities, he was able to find his way to his own bed with a minimum of assistance. But just where or when he acquired the nice, big, red Soviet star he found secured next morning to the buttonhole of his jacket lapel remains a mystery to him to this day.

Unfortunately, in the higher levels of international relations events were not proceeding in the jovial and comradely style which marked the dealings between the crew of *Commando* and their hosts from the air force of the U.S.S.R. Stalin, greatly disappointed by Churchill's reluctance to agree to an early invasion of the European mainland across the English Channel, was treating the prime minister in a remarkably surly fashion. So much so that Churchill was at one point considering cutting his Moscow visit short and huffily returning to London without bothering to make any further attempts to solidify the new and important relationship with the Russian ally.

Once, after one of his long night meetings with Stalin, the prime minister sat gloomily on the side of his bed contemplating the idea of abruptly returning to London on the very next day. But then, speaking half to himself, he was heard to mutter:

"We're a long way from home—four days' flight. And the journey is not without danger."

Suddenly, on the final evening of Churchill's tremendously fateful and vital visit to Moscow, the whole atmosphere surrounding his discussions with Stalin dramatically changed. Not until just before dawn on the morning of *Commando*'s scheduled takeoff from Moscow did Churchill arrive at the airport, accompanied by Foreign Minister Molotov. It was fairly evident, when the prime minister debarked from his car, that he too had been fighting the good fight in a toasting joust with the Soviet leaders, in the kind of ceremony which obviously provided, at almost any level, one of the major occupational hazards of dealing with the Russians.

Averell Harriman later described, as follows, the valiant last stand made by the prime minister on that historic occasion at Moscow:

> The next day, August 15, Churchill called on Stalin alone for a short talk and to say good-bye. It turned out to be an all night session. Stalin invited him to stay for dinner, and their talk continued for over seven hours. In fact there was only an hour or two between this meeting and our departure for Tehran at 5 A.M. Churchill was highly gratified by the intimacy of the talk, and it established the personal relationship between the two men during the war.

Still accompanied by a Russian navigator, who remained on the flight deck back to Tehran, *Commando* climbed into the early morning skies over Moscow on August 16. All aboard save the crew slumbered soundly after the rather strenuous social aspects of their mission to discuss the affairs of war with their new Russian allies.

As *Commando* thundered along through the grey early morning light—a light that, dim though it was, Vanderkloot would much rather have avoided—distant flashes and smoke in the sky up ahead denoted that an air raid was taking place. Thinking it a bad time and place to encounter one of the aircraft of the Luftwaffe, *Commando*'s skipper took pains to alter course well to the east in order to give the scene of this action as wide a berth as possible. The anti-aircraft fire soon was left far behind on the starboard side, but all hands on *Commando*'s flight deck remained tensely on the alert. Only one chance meeting with one wandering German aircraft would have brought disaster to *Commando* and a large portion of the free world that morning.

Down below, the Russian countryside was becoming warmed by the mellow rays of the rising August sun. In some respects, it looked like the familiar landscape Bill Vanderkloot had so often gazed down upon while flying over the U.S. midwest in the DC-2s, in those airline days which now seemed almost centuries ago. This huge land, which looked so deceivingly tranquil, was fighting for life in its greatest struggle since Napoleon had marched his armies to the gates of Moscow. Glancing over at his Russian navigator, Bill Vanderkloot smiled and held his hand upright, with finger and thumb curled in an okay signal. It may not have been a full, comradely Red salute, but it was good enough to bring a cheerful grin from his Soviet aide. After all, there was a fraternity of the air which could climb above the barriers of both language and politics.

The Russian's command of English was certainly scanty enough. Most of his communications were in the form of compass bearings, marked in figures from time to time on bits of paper. Although, ordinarily, such an expert aerial navigator as Vanderkloot might have found it a bit irksome to be receiving compass bearings on his own flight deck from such foreign sources, certain aspects of this journey made the presence of the Russian officers on *Commando* particularly reassuring. Not only must they give enemy-occupied territory as wide a berth as possible but it was also quite prudent to have someone aboard who could guide *Commando* safely along the narrowly prescribed routes on which the Russian anti-aircraft crews had been given ample warning of the progress of such a strange airplane. After all, in this tense region so close to the battle lines, the Russians had been known at times to open fire even on their own aircraft.

According to Harriman, he had experienced at least one such uncomfortable incident during a previous flight over the area in a Russian plane.

"On arrival in Archangel," he recalled, "we flew with a fighter escort to Moscow in two Soviet planes, copies of the American DC-3. It was a rough trip as the Russian pilots flew under the low-hanging clouds. They had no navigational aids and navigated by the lay of the land. It was literally tree top flying. And when we were shot at by a Soviet anti-aircraft battery, which had not been informed of our flight, we seemed to fly *between* the trees."

Commando's return journey to Cairo, once more by way of Tehran, went off quite smoothly. No enemy or

Russian gunfire disturbed the voyage and this time, after the stop at Tehran, *Commando*'s crew was allowed to re-enter the aircraft without hindrance from the highly conscientious Russian sentries at the airport.

Upon his arrival back in Cairo, Churchill was gratified to receive a message from the King congratulating him on the progress of his talks with Premier Stalin. While in Moscow, the prime minister had kept the War Cabinet in London closely informed. He also received a message of praise from his old and staunch friend Prime Minister Smuts, who ended his communication to Churchill with a few words of caution, "After your recent Herculean labours, I implore you to relax. You cannot continue at the present pace. Please follow Charles Wilson's advice, as you would expect the nation to follow yours."

However, as much as Churchill respected the wisdom of Smuts, he seemed to be in no mood to heed it, now that he was on the scene of action and had the bit in his teeth, far from the restrictions of Westminster and Whitehall. He insisted upon getting as close to the front as possible and would have visited "at least a forward observation post" of a sector held by some New Zealand troops had not their commander, General Bernard Freyberg, flatly turned thumbs down on the proposition. This was not a matter, the prime minister had to wryly admit, "about which orders are usually given, even by the highest authority."

Riding about in the desert in his zip suit and a wide-brimmed piece of headgear which appeared to be a kind of compromise between a ten-gallon and a five-gallon hat, Churchill was cheered lustily by the grinning, battle-hardened troops of the Eighth Army and especially by the soldiers of his old regiment, the 4th Hussars.

With the mighty Afrika Korps of General Rommel now not much more than 100 miles away, after an unbroken string of victories against the Eighth Army which had pressed the British back over hundreds of miles of desert, Cairo's mood was that of a city under seige. Even the office workers of the British forces in the city were armed and ready to take their places in the front lines in the event that Rommel managed to crash through in one final thrust that would carry him right into Cairo. Yet Churchill was obviously in "fine fettle," and pleased not only with the results of his first meeting with Stalin but also with the marked and dramatic improvement of morale among the troops that had rapidly taken place with the arrival at their head of Generals Alexander and Montgomery.

Of Alexander, Churchill admiringly remarked, "Cool, gay, comprehending all, he inspired quiet, deep confidence in every quarter."

But now, at last, it was time to climb once more aboard *Commando* for the return to London, from where he had been absent for almost three weeks. On the big Liberator, all was in readiness. During their stay in Cairo, the crew had had time to check and recheck even the smallest part and corner of the machine. The smooth beat of her engines sounded sweet indeed to the ears of her skipper as they were run up during the careful cockpit check immediately before takeoff. The sun, now glowing red, slipped down toward the desert horizon. Once more, on the long hop to Gibraltar, *Commando* would be flying mainly by night and by the stars, one more lonely speck hanging there in the skies above the vast and barren sands of North Africa. While the world awaited from the lips of Churchill an account of a historic mission which would have much to do with changing the course of the greatest war in history, he himself, for many hours yet, would be part of that other infinitely smaller world within the cabin of *Commando*. Suspended there in the limitless heavens, he was totally dependent upon the continuing and steady throb of the aircraft's four great engines and the skill of five young men on its flight deck. Should either the men or the machine falter or fail in their passage across the huge and desolate wastes of the Sahara Desert, the blow to Allied hopes would be beyond calculation.

With Alexander and Montgomery standing at the airport waving Churchill farewell, *Commando* thundered down the runway, shook the blowing desert sands from her wheels, and rose gracefully into the sky. Ahead lay Gibraltar, and after that, the always dangerous crossing of the outer edge of the Bay of Biscay, before Land's End once more came into comforting view.

On the morning after *Commando*'s departure from Cairo, Churchill was a trifle tardy in showing up in his zipsuit on the aircraft's flight deck to resume his duties in the co-pilot's seat, a chore which usually began promptly at the crack of dawn. Churchill recorded:

We sailed from the Desert airfield at 7 P.M. on August 23, and I slept the sleep of the just till long after daylight. When I clambered along the bomb bay to the cockpit of the "Commando" we were already approaching Gibraltar. I must say it looked very dangerous. All was swathed in morning mist. One could not see a hundred yards ahead, and we were not flying more than thirty feet above the sea. I asked Vanderkloot if it was all right, and I said I hoped he would not hit the Rock of Gibraltar. His answers were not particularly reassuring, but he felt sufficiently sure of his course not to go up high and stand out to sea, which personally I would have been glad to see him do. We held on for another four or five minutes. Then suddenly we flew into clear air, and up towered the great precipice of Gibraltar, gleaming on the isthmus and strip of neutral ground which joins it to Spain and the mountain called the Queen of Spain's Chair. After three or four hours' flying in mist, Vanderkloot had been exact. We passed the grim rock-face a few hundred yards away without having to alter course, and made a perfect landing.

But even this superb display of airmanship did not completely subdue at least a lingering remnant of professional criticism in the thoughts of Bill Vanderkloot's illustrious temporary co-pilot, always so keenly mindful of his responsibilities on the flight deck.

"I still think it would have been better to go aloft and circle around for an hour or two," Churchill added in his memoirs. "We had the petrol and were not pressed for time. But it was a fine performance."

Commando taxied jauntily toward the tarmac along

the Gibraltar runway, with its big engines snorting and bellowing triumphantly, after the manner of some giant and hoarsely-crowing black fighting cock that had just won another long, hard battle. Bill Vanderkloot once more found himself directing an uneasy sidelong glance toward that curious tower in the "neutral" territory just across the border where, as usual, binoculars were already being trained on *Commando* by some highly interested spectators.

On that same day, after being serviced at Gibraltar, *Commando* continued on her journey to England. Crossing the Bay of Biscay, a critical portion of the route, Vanderkloot made as wide a detour out to sea as possible. The Bay of Biscay was known to be a favorite prowling ground for Messerschmitt 109 fighter aircraft from the Luftwaffe base at Biarritz in southern France. The *Commando,* with her pitifully inadequate armament, was not meant to fight, but to elude the enemy at all times by every possible means. For this reason, Vanderkloot had no desire to be any nearer than hundreds of miles from German aircraft. Fate would have it otherwise. Later, as he flew from Cairo to London with another great personage in the British war effort, he would nearly become, for a few hair-raising minutes, much too well-acquainted with the Luftwaffe fighters.

But on this flight the perilous crossing of the Bay of Biscay was accomplished without incident, and before long *Commando* was nearing the south coast of England.

On the last leg of her approach to Lyneham airport, *Commando* was picked up by an escort of Spitfires. Although Captain Vanderkloot appreciated the honor being accorded his aircraft and her distinguished passengers, he wasn't particularly pleased. He preferred to have the big black bomber fly always alone and at night—the darker the night and the more alone the better. The sight of the swift escort of Spitfires streaking across the great shining disk of the full moon that was rising over England that evening vaguely disturbed him, because such hustle and bustle could attract the attention of enemy aircraft. Bill Vanderkloot felt immensely relieved on that evening of Monday, August 24, 1942, when *Commando* rolled to a stop on the tarmac, her door opened and Prime Minister Churchill returned once more to the protection of normal security. He had been flown through 15,000 miles of perilous skies with his safety lying mainly in the hands of two young Americans and three young Canadians; and with the entire Luftwaffe longing for one good, clean shot at the big aircraft they knew was carrying Winston Churchill—but never quite when or where.

After her Moscow flight, *Commando*'s crew proudly decorated her fuselage with a hammer-and-sickle symbol within a red star, to mark the great occasion. A short time later, a sterling silver matchbox initialled "W.S.C. to W.J.V." was sent by Churchill to Bill Vanderkloot as a memento of their great and highly successful adventure. Bill noted, with a grin, that the prime minister, apparently willing to accept the Soviets as allies in such times of dire emergency, couldn't quite bring himself to be a party to this hammer-and-sickle nonsense when it came to buying a personal gift for his pilot.

Instead of the familiar Soviet insignia, the matchbox bore the old Imperial Russian eagle of the Czars, flanked by the British lion! The souvenir had to have *some* kind of Russian association to be a meaningful reminder of the historic occasion. But Winston Churchill, the dedicated Royalist, quite obviously was determined it should never be the symbol of the Bolshevik rascals whom he had so long and heartily despised.

Chapter Seventeen

C hurchill's triumphant return from the long and eventful trip to Cairo and Moscow which had accomplished such a great deal in reorganizing the high command in North Africa and achieving what appeared to be a new solidarity with the Soviet ally, naturally received a large amount of worldwide attention in the newspapers and on the radio. Somewhat to their surprise, and with a certain amount of discomfort, the crew of *Commando* found themselves the objects of a rather dazzling glare of publicity. Although it would seem natural for heroes to appreciate kudos for a job well done, it came almost as second nature to the team that flew *Commando* to stay out of the limelight. It was their wish to do their job as quietly as possible. Having their pictures plastered all over the front pages of the newspapers in both North America and Great Britain made them uneasy, because undoubtedly there were those who had more than a mere passing curiosity about what they looked like. It wasn't a case of false modesty. It was more a matter of self-preservation.

However, they were now celebrities and there wasn't much they could do about it. Movie stars Ben Lyon and his wife Bebe Daniels came into London from their home in the country to pay them a visit, and brought along a couple of dozen fresh eggs for them. The famed radio commentator Edward R. Murrow, whose superb wartime broadcasts from London were listened to so avidly by millions in the United States and Canada, interviewed them on his show.

Not long after their return from the flight to Cairo and Moscow, Bill Vanderkloot and co-pilot Jack Ruggles were given the high honor of being invited out to Chequers, the country residence of British prime ministers, to spend the weekend as guests of their distinguished passenger. They were accompanied on the drive down from London by the Right Honorable Harold Balfour, under secretary of state for Air, a pleasant man who had himself been a fighter pilot and the winner of a Military Cross in the First World War.

As their car drove through the open gates of the beautiful estate on the mellow September morning, Vanderkloot and Ruggles found themselves approaching the impressive Chequers mansion, experiencing more nervous apprehension than ever before—even while making a crosswind landing in *Commando* on the cramped Gibraltar airstrip. On the flight deck of the Liberator they were, loosely speaking, on home ground, where they could feel a little more at ease with even such a personage as the prime minister. But this was entirely different territory.

It was soon evident, however, when they reached the awesome portals of Chequers, that their misgivings had been somewhat exaggerated. The door was opened to them by none other than the familiar Sawyers. By now he seemed like an old friend after having treated *Commando's* crew to so many welcome tea breaks in the cockpit, during the long voyage to and from Moscow. Sawyers ushered the visitors into a study to join Mr. Churchill and his charming wife Clementine.

The prime minister gave them an extremely warm welcome and sat chatting in casual fashion for some time until he finally had to leave to confer with Balfour.

That evening after dinner, with a fire crackling merrily in the hearth, Churchill, comfortably clad in pajamas, dressing gown and his impressive blue velvet slippers with the "P.M." embroidered on the toes, sipped several night caps. He paced back and forth discussing the progress of the war and numerous other topics, from the reliability of the Soviet ally to English women and English horses. The Russians he regarded still with considerable suspicion. As for English women and English horses, they were both the most beautiful in the world, except that, for some strange reason, neither seemed to "do very well, once they are taken out of the country."

The prime minister was in such fine fettle that evening that it wasn't until nearly two o'clock in the morning that Vanderkloot and Ruggles went up to their bedroom. Their pajamas has been neatly arranged beside their pillows by the attentive Sawyers, who was back on hand again first thing next morning with another fresh, hot pot of tea for them.

Obviously, Sawyers had taken as great a liking for *Commando*'s crew as they had taken for him. Vanderkloot and Ruggles, being Americans, appeared to particularly interest Churchill's nimble and obliging little valet. His eyes, peering out at them from under pale blond lashes, often twinkled as he responded to some of their questions. Americans somehow delighted and amused him. As for Vanderkloot and Ruggles, they were equally fascinated by a genuine English gentleman's gentleman who appeared to have all the sterling qualities, and then some, of P. G. Wodehouse's fabled Jeeves.

In addition to this, they all shared a special kind of bond that came from an abiding desire to preserve and protect, in their own ways, the comfort and safety of the great man who carried so well upon his shoulders the immense burdens of such a high office in such fateful times. Sawyers had long ago become familiar with the human side of Churchill, the renowned world figure. And Vanderkloot and Ruggles were gaining their own personal kind of knowledge of the prime minister's more off-guard moods and foibles. His frequent visits to *Commando*'s flight deck, were charged with a certain kind of drama that was peculiarly capable of compressing the equivalent of days or even weeks of more casual association into comparatively brief intervals.

It was a pleasant and restful interlude, that first of two weekend visits to Chequers, being shown about the great mansion and the beautiful grounds surrounding it by Churchill himself. Once he paused beside a wall and pointed up to a bird's nest in one of the openings among the stones.

"That nest," he explained, "was once occupied by a sparrow, sitting hopefully on her eggs. One day a cuckoo arrived and layed an egg among those of the poor sparrow, who kept right on sitting over them until they hatched. As the small birds began to grow up, that little sparrow seemed to be particularly proud of what she thought was her largest and lustiest off-spring. But then the day arrived when this large member of the brood set about tossing its smaller companions out of the nest, after being nursed to such robust state by that small mother bird.

"It almost reminds one," said Churchill, with a wry smile, "of what's beginning to happen to us in India."

On Sunday afternoon, after a fond farewell from their host and recent companion in great adventure, Bill Vanderkloot and Jack Ruggles were driven back to London, and the awaiting *Commando*. Shortly after, the big black Liberator was flown up to Prestwick and thence back across the wide North Atlantic to Gander and on to her home base at Dorval to await her next special assignment.

Between such missions, Bill Vanderkloot was kept busy in many other ways carrying out important chores for Ferry Command. In November of 1942, Vanderkloot was awarded the Order of the British Empire, which he received at Rideau Hall in Ottawa from the hands of Canada's Governor General, the Earl of Athlone.

The citation described the award as being "for outstanding work as an accurate instrument pilot and specialist in radio range work; being instrumental in assisting with all radio facilities for Ferry Command in the United Kingdom and for making all final arrangements for ferrying aircraft over the South Atlantic."

Vanderkloot thought then of his sidekick Duke Schiller and how they had spent so many nights on the rooftop of an apartment house in Montreal, painfully learning the tricks of celestial navigation. Now they were paying off in more ways than one for the quiet young American who approached his hazardous profession with a passion for thoroughness that embraced the most minute detail of aerial pilotage.

Back in the Tower Apartments in Montreal, Bill Vanderkloot was from time to time reunited—for a usually all-too-brief period—with his wife Della and their small daughter Patricia. Della, a striking Irish blonde, had been a professional dancer before their marriage. She had, in fact, once performed in the pre-war days before none other than Adolf Hitler when the German dictator happened to pay a surprise visit to a theatre where she was appearing in Vienna. Bill sometimes teased her about how her old admirer was making it so difficult for him to carry out his chores on the far side of the Atlantic. Della worried a lot about her husband's hazardous occupation, but tried her best to conceal it during those short reunions, so that he could relax and enjoy a little domestic bliss between assignments. As for Patricia, she had come to look upon her father's far-ranging perambulations as a fairly normal kind of life, not so much different from that of the travelling salesman father of one of her chums in the Tower Apartments.

Sometimes when she answered a telephone call for her father she'd casually reply, "I think Daddy's in Africa some place today, but we're expecting him home tomorrow or the next day."

Yet with all of their comparative tranquility far from the scenes of war, and occupied by the same kind of people you'd expect to find in any similar place in Montreal, the Tower Apartments were hit by tragedy and despair on numerous occasions. Several Ferry Command aircrew members lived in the building. In one single day the dreaded news arrived that four different families in the apartments had lost their husbands or fathers in aircraft crashes.

The tragedies struck with numbing suddenness, and almost always the big ones occurred on the Return Ferry, when a planeload of aircrews on their way back to Dorval plunged into some hillside in Scotland or Newfoundland. On one occasion a memorial service was being held in a Montreal church for more than a score of Ferry Command air crew members who had just been lost on a return flight to Canada. The minister had to interrupt the proceedings to announce from the pulpit that still another crash had occurred, taking the lives of an equal number of men, some of whose families were assembled in the church that day to mourn the loss of their friends and neighbors.

The Ferry Command losses during the course of its operations, took away some of the oldest hands and some of the newest. Flying Officer H. W. Oldham, for example, was killed on his first Ferry Command flight. In March of 1942, Captain R. Humphrey Page, (one of the trio of old Imperial Airways hands that included Captains I. G. Ross and D. C. T. Bennett), a man who helped lay the original foundations of the Ferry Command operations, lost his life when his ferry aircraft was shot down on the other side of the Atlantic. Within a week after the announcement of his death, the body of his widow was found in the kitchen of their Montreal apartment, the gas jets of the stove turned on and the windows and doors stuffed with paper.

Other Allied airmen in other services were, of course, paying the same awful price of war while the Ferry Command crews were losing their lives. But there was something particularly nerve-wracking about the alternate periods of living comparatively normal existences for a few days with their families in Montreal, and then going far away once more to face death and danger. It placed a peculiar extra strain upon the aircrews of Ferry Command, and was a kind of life that didn't provide much time to become fully hardened to peril. So much repeated switching back and forth between the normal and the nightmarish didn't really allow these men to adjust to either one life or the other. The rapid contrasts seemed to keep them constantly suspended between two strange worlds which didn't have any reasonable relation to each other. There was something unreal about having a few friends in for dinner one night, or reading a bedtime story to a youngster in the safe haven of Montreal; and then setting out on the very next morning, before the first cold light of dawn, to fly across the wide North Atlantic on what might be—and what was for so many—the final mission.

Occasionally there were seemingly miraculous incidents which restored to the Montreal community of flying men some of its members for whom all hope had been abandoned after their names had been posted for several days upon the grim list of the missing.

One of the strangest of these deliverances from the dead involved the three-man crew of a Hampden bomber being ferried from England to Canada in the later stages of the war to serve at one of the training schools on this side of the Atlantic. By then these schools were turning out large numbers of aircrews under what was called the British Commonwealth Air Training Plan. Canada's wide spaces and location far from the theatres of war made the country ideal for the operation of such a huge enterprise.

Captain Robert E. Coffman of Louisiana, Flying Officer Norman E. Greenaway, R.C.A.F., of Alberta and Radio Officer Ronald E. Snow of Digby, Nova Scotia, headed out from England in their battle-scarred bomber to fly the Iceland-Labrador route to Canada. Two hours out from Iceland on the second and final leg of their journey across the lower portion of the lonely roof of the world, just as they were approaching the rugged coast of Greenland, one of the Hampden's two 980 h.p. Bristol engines failed. After limping along on one engine for the better part of an hour, during which time the aircraft dropped from an altitude of 9,000 feet down to 4,500, the bomber staggered into a spin. Captain Coffman managed to regain control at about a thousand feet above the sea, but after a few minutes the remaining engine completely died. The Hampden had to be ditched upon an ocean so cruelly frigid that a man could expect to live for only a few minutes if he were forced to swim in its waters. On the way down to the landing on the sub-Arctic sea, Radio Officer Snow managed to tap out an S.O.S., but radio conditions that day were such that the "skip" of his transmission carried it over and past the usual wireless listening posts. They went down in that tremendous isolation without providing the slightest clue concerning their last position.

Although the Hampden rolled over and sank only seventy seconds after smacking down into the sea, its crew managed to scramble into an inflated dinghy with a kit of emergency rations. They were about fifteen miles off the shore of Greenland; all around them extended great fields of pack ice. A somewhat astonished seal surfaced nearby for a few moments, took a startled look at the occupants of the dinghy, then submerged with an indifferent slap of its flippers after the wet and shivering Snow enquired: "Where's the North Pole, Daddy?" Later, he was to regret that joke. If, instead of asking jaunty questions, he or the others had managed to bag the animal, they would not have missed the one chance in their whole terrible eleven-day ordeal of eating a solid meal.

For the first twenty hours, until ten o'clock next morning, they paddled and pushed their way through and around the ice floes until they reached land—not the actual Greenland coast, but a huge black rock rising some 3,000 feet high, not far off the island's shore. After observing the powerful current swirling between the rock and the island, they realized they could never navigate their flimsy rubber dinghy across the final gap that lay between them and Greenland. Instead, they decided to seek refuge somewhere on the face of the great rock.

The only perch they could find on its cold surface consisted of a narrow ledge about one hundred feet above the surface of the sea. There was not a stick of firewood or vegetation on it of any kind. Setting up the deflated dinghy as a kind of tent, they took stock of their resources: one Very pistol with twenty-seven cartridges; three containers holding forty-five malted milk tablets; four squares of barley sugar; a few sticks of chewing gum; twelve sealed pints of drinking water; a first aid kit; a yellow distress flag; and a four-inch square metal mirror with an attachment that permitted it to be used as a heliograph. Huddled there for the first two days in driving snow and sleet, they rationed themselves at first to a third of a pint of water and six malted milk tablets per day. The blizzards were followed by two days of sub-zero weather which froze their wet flying suits as stiff as boards. Then came three days of furious gales, which blew away their pathetic, small, yellow distress flag and sent the cold and angry seas leaping so high against the face of the rock that they painfully had to crawl up to another ledge, 250 feet farther above the water.

On the ninth day a passing ship was sighted about fifteen miles away, but with a heavy cloud layer obscuring the sun they could not use the heliograph. Six shots from their Very pistol fired at five-minute intervals evidently escaped the notice of those on the bridge of the vessel, and it finally disappeared beyond the murky horizon. By now convinced that they were surely to die upon this rock, the men discussed what messages should be left for their families, in case their bodies were ever found. But what paper they had was soggy pulp and anyway, their hands were too numb and cold to properly hold a pencil even if the paper were dry.

They began to occupy their minds with ridiculously simple things as they crouched there in their small, bleak world so far from their fellow men.

"Someone," Captain Coffman later recalled, "drew attention to the fact that each of us had a middle name beginning with the letter 'E'; we thought that was an extraordinary coincidence and talked childishly about it for ever so long. We were desperately hungry but never mentioned the fact, only reciting to each other stories of steaks and other foods we had eaten when delivering bombers to different parts of the world. When one of us dropped off in a coma for awhile, he would mention on waking that he had been dreaming about gargantuan meals in which dumplings and thick gravy always seemed to figure. We saw no prospect of rescue, but we made a point of taking a vow every few minutes that we would never again complain about food, even the abundance of carrots which we get every time we fly to Britain. Every few minutes we were also speaking mournfully about the sea-lion which came out of the sea to see us off at the start of our voyage, and whose blubber and meat would have been a godsend to us."

At noon on the eleventh day, the radio officer crawled out of the ledge to get a handful of snow with which to quench their increasingly unbearable thirst. He was greatly excited as he crawled back under the scanty shelter of the dinghy.

"Say, boys, I'm awful queer and may be seeing things," he hoarsely whispered, "but I think there's a ship out there, standing still."

Pushing aside the cover of the dinghy, his companions stared out to sea, and beheld a small two-masted vessel, stopped about eight miles away. This cheering sight was followed by another: the long-absent sun suddenly broke out from behind the clouds and continued to shine for the next three hours as the stranded men desperately worked their heliograph and fired the last of their Very pistol cartridges.

It so happened that what they had at first thought was some kind of mirage born of delirium was a converted whaler named the *Polar Bjorn,* carrying a Norwegian crew and several U.S. Army officers proceeding to a post in Greenland. By a million-to-one chance, the *Polar Bjorn* had been forced to hove to at that particular spot in that vast and otherwise deserted expanse of ice and water while repairs were made to a faulty engine. Another peculiar coincidence—the kind that might be scoffed at in fiction but sometimes happens in real life—was the fact that while the *Polar*

Bjorn's engineers were tinkering about below decks on the vessel's engines, a U.S. army major decided to go outside with his binoculars to have a look at Greenland's forbidding coastline. His fortunate decision was made near the end of three hours of frantic signalling from the stranded airmen. Their high hopes had begun to sink back into despair as no one aboard the *Polar Bjorn* had yet noticed the firing of their few remaining, precious Very pistol cartridges and the flashing of their heliograph. Even the major thought he must be mistaken when he finally perceived a flash from the mirror. He decided it must have been a glint from a piece of snow or ice on the great black rock. Then he saw what looked like a small puff of smoke in the sky and a quick, bright flash which he imagined might be a seagull wheeling on its white wings in the sun. But when this object (which was Captain Coffman's last Very cartridge) abruptly plummeted into the cold grey sea, he concluded it couldn't have been a gull and began to focus his glasses more closely on the rock. It was then that he observed what had to be signals flashing from a mirror.

When the Major informed the Norwegian captain of his strange discovery, the skipper at first was quite leery. He believed it might either be some trick of a German submarine trying to lure them closer to shore, or a ruse by some Nazi agents who might have set up a radio station on the rock.

"Then let's go and capture them!" suggested the courageous major. A small boat was launched, bearing the major and three Norwegian seamen armed with automatic rifles and with knives tucked into their belts. When they came within range, they trained their rifles on the rocky ledge. But they quickly lowered them again when they discovered the rock occupied by three weak and almost dead airmen. The exhausted men were taken aboard the *Polar Bjorn,* wrapped in warm blankets, and bedded down in a snug cabin where they almost immediately fell asleep. Meanwhile, the *last boat* of the season to navigate that particular ice-flecked channel continued on her way to her destination in Greenland. Such was the saga of one Ferry Command crew, who by such a miraculously narrow margin, cheated death on the long and lonely run across the North Atlantic.

Chapter Eighteen

As the war progressed and the campaigns in the South Pacific began to make more demands upon the services of Ferry Command, Bill Vanderkloot and some of his comrades who had been flying the dismal North Atlantic route sometimes found themselves operating in much more benevolent winter weather. But there were certain drawbacks which tended to cancel out the advantages of flying in such salubrious climes. The Pacific was, after all, a much larger ocean than the Atlantic, with all of its mean moods. Landing spots on the Pacific were often few, small and far between.

The slightest error in navigation could cause an aircraft of Ferry Command to miss a destination which might consist of only one tiny islet. These islands formed small but vital stepping stones in the long aerial trail that led across the great body of water lying between the North American mainland and such points as Australia, New Zealand or Ceylon.

One Ferry Command skipper who was particularly experienced in the ways of the Pacific when the service began operations in that large part of the globe was the American pilot Clyde Pangborn. In 1931 with Hugh Herndon, he had carried out the first nonstop flight across that wide ocean from Sabishiro Beach, Japan, to Wenatchee, Washington. So heavily loaded with fuel was their Bellanca monoplane that they had to rig up a method of jettisoning their landing gear immediately after takeoff to help reduce the drag of wind resistance, retractable gear not being available for such aircraft at that time. They had completed the epic trans-Pacific flight in forty-one hours and thirteen minutes, landing the Bellanca on its belly when they reached Wenatchee. Now, Pangborn was helping to deliver the bombers which would contribute to the eventual defeat of the country where he had begun his historic flight ten years earlier.

When Captain Vanderkloot began to fly the South Pacific run, he discovered a peculiar and helpful phenomenon. It came in handy when trying to achieve the pinpoint kind of navigation necessary to find your way through that vast expanse of ocean to the haven of a landing strip on some tiny island. Often, long before the island itself came into view, a single cloud could be seen far in the distance hanging over it in an otherwise clear blue sky. Such welcome markers were created by the rising currents of warmer air ascending from the small blob of land into the cooler levels of the upper atmosphere. The navigator, engaged in a precise kind of shooting match where one near miss could be fatal found this characteristic of the tropics and sub-tropics helpful indeed in trying to hit the bullseye.

In those days, not enough time had elapsed since the Japanese attack on Pearl Harbour to allow the U.S. to fully organize its communications and other facilities in the vast Pacific. Thus, the crews ferrying military aircraft from North America to Australia, New Zealand and the Far East often encountered strange sights while island-hopping across the great ocean. On one journey to deliver a Mitchell bomber to the hard-pressed Dutch East Indies, Bill Vanderkloot's flight route carried him from California to Hawaii and thence southward to diminutive Canton Island, a mere speck on the face of the broad Pacific. This island served as a refueling point for. aircraft being flown to distant scenes of operation.

When Vanderkloot landed the Mitchell on the rather cramped and crude little Canton Island airstrip, he was greeted by the commanding officer of one of the most forlorn looking outposts of the U.S. Air Force that possibly could be imagined. Its strength consisted of a handful of officers and enlisted men and about six fighter aircraft. The planes were there and the men were there and the fuel was there—but on the entire island there were no buildings in which the men of this unit could be sheltered. They were still living in the large packing cases in which their aircraft had been delivered by ship some months earlier. Someone in the vast network of military bureaucracy, which then extended from the Pentagon in Washington around the world in rather haphazard manner, had goofed in the matter of providing living quarters for this small and comparatively insignificant military establishment. The men and the fighting equipment had arrived all right, like a kind of package deal from a mail order house. But day after day and week after week, the ship that was supposed to come to set up the shelters failed to show up at Canton Island.

Although the packing cases were fairly roomy as packing cases go, they made extremely crowded and uncomfortable dwellings. This dismal situation was not alleviated at all by the lively activities of the great and aggressive legions of huge, white, land crabs which had been the sole inhabitants of Canton Island before the U.S. Air Force took over. These crabs were utterly fearless. If a mere human approached them they refused to scurry away, but instead raised their great pincers in belligerent fashion and squared off ready to do battle and hold their ground. It reached the point where the men who seemed to have been deserted on Canton Island generally agreed that fighting the Japanese would be a cinch compared to the daily conflicts they had to endure with those big white crabs.

For one thing, articles of human attire held a particular attraction for Canton Island's original settlers. Shirts, boots, underwear and trousers were constantly and eerily taking off on their own from the packing case shelters, moving away in mysterious fashion across the sands toward the sea. As a result, the air force men were racing off incessantly to retrieve their belongings from the claws of some water-bound crab.

At first, the men on Canton Island attempted to do battle to the death with the marauders instead of merely wrestling with them all the time. But this bold tactic was quickly given up. They discovered that Canton Island being so small and the crabs being so huge and numerous, it was folly to kill them because there was no way of getting rid of the horrible smell of their rotting carcases lying about in the hot sun. Even when they were killed and hurled out into the ocean, they drifted ashore again to create an almost unbearable stink all over the midget island. So the contest between Canton Island's crabs and the U.S. Air Force had merely deteriorated into a kind of miserable snatch-and-grab-back stalemate.

On another occasion, when Vanderkloot landed on Christmas Island, he found an equally curious situation which again illustrated how the men of an isolated and almost forgotten military outpost, far out on the great bosom of the Pacific, could be frustrated and even tormented by flaws in the hastily established communications and transportation facilities which at that time extended over that vast area.

Christmas Island, it turned out, was manned by one U.S. Air Force captain and a dozen enlisted men and equipped with two fighter aircraft, some tents, some rifles, two rather stunted palm trees and 5,000 cases of Coca Cola. The captain mournfully explained to Bill Vanderkloot how his humble unit had been so overly blessed by this fantastic supply of soft drinks. He had taken to brooding, some weeks earlier, about the slim chances he and his men would have in attempting to hold this minute strip of sand far out in the lonely Pacific should some wandering Japanese submarine or other hostile vessel launch an attack upon it. So he sent off a coded wireless message one day containing an urgent request for reinforcements. Somewhere, along the tortuous path of communications which led from Christmas Island to the proper military authorities, the word "reinforcements" became decoded into "refreshments." This explained why a ship arrived over the horizon one day to discharge a cargo of Coke capable of slaking the thirsts of a large part of the military establishment of Honolulu for a considerable period.

"If the Japs arrive here tomorrow or the next day," remarked the Captain, with a gloomy sigh, "we won't even have a single machine gun to fight them off. But we'll sure as hell be able to offer them a drink when they come ashore!"

At some of these island airstrips located along the staging routes which extended across the Pacific, the mosquitoes were renowned for their size and ferocity.

One story had it that two mosquitoes were hauling a burly pilot out of his tent when one of them was plainly heard to say, "Let's just drag him down to the swamp where we can eat him in comfort."

To which the other replied, "Nothing doing! The big fellows down there would take him away from us."

And there was a mechanic on Canton Island who swore to Vanderkloot that one mosquito which happened to land on the lonely airstrip one evening was so big that he and his mates had poured 100 gallons of gasoline into it before they discovered it wasn't a west-bound bomber.

Things got better on these lonely landing spots far out on the Pacific as the war progressed and more aircraft streamed from North American plants across the ocean to destinations such as Australia and New Zealand. Sometimes the Ferry Command crews could enjoy the luxury of a layover in an Australian hotel in Sydney or Melbourne. Such pleasant intervals were often, of course, marked by a certain amount of convivial wine and song. One night in their Sydney hotel room, Ferry Command Captain Jack Sharp and some other civilian pilots were engaged in this jolly pastime when they learned that none other than General Douglas McArthur was a fellow guest in the establishment. At that time the war was going quite badly for the Allies in the Pacific. This sad fact was discussed more and more moodily by the gathering of pilots in

Jack Sharp's room as the evening wore on and the liquor supply dwindled.

Finally Sharp walked to the telephone, called the switchboard, and curtly requested to be put through to the general's suite. Perhaps because the call originated within the hotel or perhaps because the operator was particularly obliging, it did go through, and McArthur was brought to the phone.

"General," he said, "this is Captain Jack Sharp of the R.A.F. Ferry Command speaking. We've had quite a discussion on this matter and my mates and I have agreed that we sure don't like the way you're running the war out here in the Pacific. . . . We're losing all over the damned place!"

The move to another hotel, at the urgent request of the management, was made by Sharp and his pals within the half hour, just in time to prevent one member of the gathering from giving still another demonstration of one of his pet and rather intriguing theories: if a man on foot could achieve sufficient momentum, by racing fast enough around and around a room, centrifugal force would at one point permit him to run right up the wall for a modest distance. This "skill" could gradually be improved with proper training and fuel of the right octane rating. Once, this man was said to have achieved before witnesses an altitude of almost three feet above floor level in a room of the Mount Royal Hotel before stalling and crashing to the carpet.

Hop-off point for the trans-Pacific flights was usually Hamilton Field in San Francisco and sometimes the layover there lasted long enough for Bill Vanderkloot and other pilots of Ferry Command to avail themselves of the lavish hospitality of Dr. Margaret "Mom" Chung. Mom, who it's said was the prototype for "Ma Jong," the warm-hearted Chinese lady of the comic strip "Terry and the Pirates," was a wealthy woman who had been stricken with an acute case of hero worship for all submarine and airplane crews. She had turned her impressive residence into a kind of luxurious club which she liked to think of as a

151

home away from home for her large family of boys. The doors were always open to them, and within the walls of Mom Chung's big house they were treated like a flock of pampered children.

There was an abundance of food and liquor for all and it was a rare day or night that one of Mom's far-wandering "sons" arrived at the place and a party of some kind or other wasn't in full swing. Never was any rank recognized except those established by Mom Chung herself, and these were observed with great respect. It was not at all unusual to see an admiral standing behind the bar serving drinks or a general washing glasses. Mom even went so far as to provide for her "family" numbered silver rings which the airmen and submarine sailors wore with great pride. Each was presented with another memento in the form of a small cardboard folder which carried on its cover a sketch of Christ hovering over a sea. On the water rode a submarine, while an airplane bearing the circled star insignia of the U.S. Air Force flew overhead. The right hand of Christ was pointed in protective fashion down toward the submarine while the left hand extended up toward the airplane. Under this impressive and sacred scene Mom had penned the words, "May the Lord watch between Thee and me while we are absent, one from the other."

Inside the cover was a portrait of Mom Chung herself, wearing her most expensive ermine jacket, and under this picture of Mom gazing out fondly upon the beholder was printed, "May God always ride with you as co-pilot. May you always have blue skies, fair weather, smooth sailing and happy landings. Wherever you are, my prayers for your safety—and my love wing their way to you. Devotedly, Mom Chung."

On the opposite page of the folder Mom had printed the "qualifications" which admitted a pilot or submarine hand to her charmed circle of pampered warriors. The pilots, whom she had placed in the most favored position, were honored with the title "Fair-Haired Bastard." The person who qualified for this exalted rank was described by Mom in her folder as "a good guy, who can fly, who's not afraid to die, a courageous man who is loyal, tolerant, a "square" man who contributes to the progress and glory of aviation, who makes the world a better place because he lives."

Next in the order of rank bestowed by Mom Chung upon her guests was the "Kiwi," who was described in her folder as "Exceptionally good 'Bastard' material, but who does not fly." Then, came Mom's Order of the Golden Dolphin, the holder of which was described as "one whose heroic and meritorious service in action distinguishes him as a man of outstanding valor, exceptional courage, unswerving loyalty and tolerance, one who contributes to the glory of the Submarine Service of the U.S. Navy, and who makes the world a finer place because he lives."

Certainly the world, at least temporarily, became a finer place in which to live for those who, having met Mom's high standards, were accepted into the privileged family of fly-boys and submariners, and who were lucky enough to spend some of their off hours in the big house overlooking San Francisco Bay. Mom Chung's name was spoken with great affection in many far-off corners of the globe, wherever members of her spoiled and cherished brood happened to cross trails.

The title of Fair-Haired Bastard, highest honor that could be received under Mom's hospitable roof, was bestowed only upon pilots because they were the ones that she, a single lady, chose to regard as her own favorite sons.

Passing through San Francisco while flying to or from some distant part of the world, a pilot had only to call Mom Chung on the telephone and announce "Mom? This is Fair-Haired Bastard Number 309. Is it okay to drop over for a while?" By the time her roving boy had reached Mom Chung's doorway, she was standing there ready to receive him in a motherly embrace and to call him affectionately by name as he stepped over the threshold.

On one flight out into the Pacific in the later stages of the war, Bill Vanderkloot carried in *Commando* Admiral Sir Bruce Fraser, Commander-in-Chief, British

Fleet in the Pacific. The admiral's mission was to confer with U.S. Admiral Ernest J. King just before the American invasion of Luzon in the Phillipines. The long flight was made from San Francisco by way of Hawaii and the Fiji Islands to Sydney, Australia and thence northwest to Leyte in the Phillipines. Although *Commando* had by this time acquired somewhat improved sleeping facilities, the aircraft still contained just one big cabin. Among Admiral Fraser's staff on the journey were two quite attractive Wrens who served as secretaries. When the Wrens were ready to retire they were too modest to undress and get into their sleeping attire in the same cabin with the admiral and other members of the official party, even with the lights out. However, for some mysterious reason, they seemed to feel more at ease while making these rather intimate changes of costume right up on the flight deck with Bill Vanderkloot and the other members of his crew. During these delicate intervals, the crew of *Commando,* to their credit, gazed ahead steadfastly at their instrument panels and carefully conversed with each other only out of the corners of their mouths, while the big aircraft droned its way westward across the Pacific.

Reaching the Phillipine island of Leyte, the *Commando* was landed on the aerodrome at Tacloben, and Admiral Fraser and the other passengers were discharged while U.S. fighter aircraft roared in and out at a furious rate. Dog tired and yearning for a shower, *Commando*'s crew looked forward to a little respite but it was not to be, so close to a combat zone. They were ordered to fly the big Liberator out of Tacloben immediately, because it would have been a prime target for the Japanese aircraft which were constantly strafing the field. After a hurried refueling, *Commando* was taken aloft again with instructions that she proceed southward on a long and wearisome flight to Noeumfoor in the Halmaheras, which lay off the coast of Netherlands New Guinea.

This island was one of those which had been bypassed by the U.S. forces, who had cut off the Japanese garrison from all supplies and simply left them to wither on the vine. Several hundred of these hungry and tattered Japanese soldiers hiding out in the jungle were no longer able to challenge the small garrison of Australian troops who then held the island. The Japanese field hospital on Noeumfoor and the nurses were allowed to move about freely and share the rations of the Australians, who, were still there. In fact, even a couple of Japanese soldiers had managed somehow to come out of the bush and ingratiate themselves with the Australians to the point where, while waiting in a chow line one day, the crew of *Commando* was startled to see standing right there ahead of them one of Hirohito's warriors with his plate held hopefully at the ready!

But the fugitives still in the bush who preferred the hardships of hiding to the shame of surrender had a much rougher time of it. The word on Noeumfoor was that the inhabitants, who were extremely handy with the bow and arrow, were being paid one guilder apiece for every Japanese ear brought in from the jungle.

Chapter Nineteen

Early in January of 1943, word came to the R.A.F. Ferry Command headquarters in Dorval that *Commando* was to be made ready and flown to England to carry out another top-secret mission. Although the name of the important person she would be carrying was by no means being bandied about, it soon became evident to Bill Vanderkloot and his crew that "the Boss" was about to go flying again.

Upon *Commando's* arrival in England, her captain was informed that Churchill was indeed to be his passenger once more. This time the prime minister's party would include Sir Charles Portal, chief of the Royal Air Force, who had selected Vanderkloot in the first place to carry out these particularly critical assignments. Their destination: Casablanca, for what was to be the historic meeting between Churchill and President Franklin D. Roosevelt.

Commando took off from an aerodrome near Oxford on January 12. In an effort to protect Churchill and his party from the chills and drafts of a flight at high altitudes in mid-winter, a makeshift auxiliary heating system had been rather hastily installed in the big Liberator. But it didn't work out quite as well as was expected and ended up, much to the embarrassment of Bill Vanderkloot and his crew, in giving the illustrious leader of the British Empire's war effort a rather severe hotfoot! Churchill later recalled:

> My journey by air was a little anxious. In order to heat the *"Commando"* they had established a petrol engine

inside which generated fumes and raised various heating-points to very high temperatures. I was woken up at two in the morning, when we were over the Atlantic five hundred miles from anywhere, by one of these heating-points burning my toes, and it looked to me as if it might soon get red-hot and burn the blankets. I therefore climbed out of my bunk, and woke up Peter Portal, who was sitting well beneath, asleep in his chair, and drew his attention to this very hot point. We looked around the cabin and found two others, which seemed equally on the verge of becoming red hot. We then went down into the bomb alley (it was a converted bomber) and found two men industriously keeping alive this petrol heater. From every point of view I thought this was dangerous. The hot points might start a conflagration, and the atmosphere of petrol would make an explosion imminent. Portal took the same view. I decided it was better to freeze than burn, and ordered all heating to be turned off, and went back to rest shivering in the ice-cold winter air about eight thousand feet up, at which we had to fly above the clouds. I am bound to say this struck me as a rather unpleasant moment.

Churchill's hotfoot and the subsequent chilly aftermath of the shut down of *Commando*'s makeshift heating plant evidently made such an impression upon her passengers that even his physician, Sir Charles Wilson, considered the incident worthy of special mention in the diary he kept of the trip. He wrote in an entry for January 13, the day of their arrival in Casablanca:

The P.M. is full of zest, though the night was not a success. In the stern of the bomber there were two mattresses, stretched side by side, one for the P.M. and one for me. The rest of the party slept in their chairs. I woke with a start to find the P.M. crawling down into the well beneath, where Portal was asleep. When he shook him vigorously by the shoulder, I thought it would be well to find out what was wrong. Winston said he had burnt his toes against some metal connections on the improvised heating arrangements at the foot of the mattress. "They are red hot," he explained. "We shall have the petrol fumes bursting into flames. There'll be an explosion soon."

Winston was thoroughly worked up about the business; the simplest thing seemed to be to turn off the heating. How long I slept after we had settled again I cannot say, but I awoke to discover the P.M. on his knees trying to keep out the draught by putting a blanket against the side of the plane. He was shivering: we were flying at 7,000 feet in an unheated bomber in mid-winter. I got up and we struggled, not with much success, to cut off the blast. An hour or two later he woke me and we returned to the attack. The P.M. is at a disadvantage in this kind of travel, since he never wears anything at night but a silk vest. On his hands and knees, he cut a quaint figure with his big, bare, white bottom.

But, shortly after first light on that morning, *Commando* slipped safely down from the sky to land in the more mellow winter climate of Casablanca. Churchill and his party were whisked away to a comfortable suburban villa near the one which would be occupied by President Roosevelt and his aides.

"The airfield near Oxford was wintry, damp and dismal," Sir Charles Wilson later recalled, "but after ten hours in the air we breakfasted in a bungalow outside Casablanca, with the sun streaming in from the blue sky and oranges, with their leaves, on our plates."

Two days after *Commando* had landed, two U.S. Army DC-4's arrived at the Casablanca airfield bearing President Roosevelt and his party. Bill Vanderkloot was surprised and delighted to find that the captain of one of these aircraft was Otis Bryan, his old chief pilot. The second aircraft was flown by Captain Milo Campbell, another longtime friend from Vanderkloot's airline days back in the U.S. It was a pleasant reunion and while the British and American leaders, with their entourages of high ranking military officers, settled down to their momentous discussions of the war and its progress, the three American skippers whose aircraft had brought them to the scene of the historic conference set out with their crews to prowl through the streets of Casablanca, rubbernecking and shopping like any other tourists. They even patronized the bar, said to have been the original version of the one in which Humphrey Bogart uttered those immortal words "Play it, Sam." That movie was to make Casablanca even more famous then did the historic wartime meeting of Roosevelt and Churchill.

With its well-treed avenues and sidewalk cafes, the North African city looked a bit like some sunny transplanted corner of Paris. Both Casablanca and its people seemed a strange mixture of modern Europe and ancient Araby. Fierce-looking bearded men of the desert, clad in flowing burnooses and yellow sandals, stalked down some street toward waiting steeds which turned out to be not camels, but sleek motor cars, drawn up at the curbside.

As for Bill Vanderkloot and his crewmates, wandering and gawking through the old and colorful city, there was one thing of which they could be fairly sure. After each excursion into Casablanca's bustling thoroughfares they usually ended up with their shoes polished to a glittering lustre. It was almost impossible to move more than half a block without having their feet grabbed by some enthusiastic and utterly dauntless sidewalk shoeshine boy who appeared to know more wrestling holds than Strangler Lewis. It made no difference if your shoes had already been shined by some tenacious urchin only fifty yards earlier. After a stroll of ten blocks or so, averaging at least two shines to the block, the footwear of *Commando's* crew acquired a truly dazzling sheen. And it didn't do much good for them to seek refuge in the chair of a sidewalk cafe when they had become exhausted from shaking off toeholds. Jack Ruggles discovered this when his weary silence, taken for consent by a passionate sidewalk cobbler, resulted in the horrifying experience of watching his brand new and highly prized pair of shoes, recently acquired from one of the better London shops, being fitted with a second pair of soles. They were hammered on with what looked like shingle nails, before he could make a move to rescue them from the cobbler's swift grasp.

At the Casablanca meeting Roosevelt and Churchill agreed upon the "unconditional surrender" terms for the Axis powers, a statement which was later to

159

create a great deal of controversy among the Allies, on the ground that it stiffened the will of the enemy to carry on, and prolonged the war. There was also the less weighty but no less frustrating and difficult matter of arranging a meeting between the French Generals Charles de Gaulle and Henri Giraud, who were then decidedly hostile toward each other. Giraud, whom the Allies had placed in command of the French forces in North Africa without what de Gaulle considered to be sufficient consultation with him, was already in Casablanca ready to make an attempt at a reconciliation with the leader of the Free French Government.

But de Gaulle, back in London, haughtily refused to join the others in Casablanca until Churchill went so far as to hint that the British government might cease to recognize him as French leader in exile if he persisted in spurning the urgent invitation from both the prime minister and the president. On January 22, de Gaulle finally showed up in Casablanca for a reluctant meeting with Giraud, an event of which Roosevelt later remarked, "We had so much trouble getting these two French generals together that I thought to myself that this was as difficult as arranging the meeting of Grant and Lee."

Turning his keen clinical eye upon the constant friction between his distinguished patient and de Gaulle, Sir Charles Wilson observed:

The P.M. is a bad hater, but in these days, when he is stretched taut, certain people seem to get on his nerves: de Gaulle is one of them. He is so stuffed with principles that there is no room left for a little Christian tolerance; in his rigidity, there is no give. Besides, men of his race do not find it easy to accept any foreigner as a superior being, and Winston does not like this kind of agnosticism.

After ten days of intensive discussion among Churchill, Roosevelt and their advisers, the president prepared to return to the United States. But Churchill wouldn't hear of it. They had been working hard. Now, he insisted, it was time for them to relax for a couple of days of rest and companionship in Marrakech, a fabled desert oasis not far away which was loved by the British leader, perhaps above all other places in Africa. It was his desire, he told Roosevelt, to be standing there beside him when first he viewed the sunset on the snows of the Atlas Mountains. For countless centuries, he explained, the caravans of Central Africa had found their way to Marrakech, to be swindled in its markets and enjoy the gay life of the city, including its fortune-tellers, snake charmers, masses of food and drink, and on the whole the largest and most elaborately organized brothels in the African continent.

"All these institutions are of long and ancient repute," said Churchill.

At any time, Churchill's oratory would have been difficult to resist. But when he really waxed poetic, as in his description of what awaited them at Marrakech, Roosevelt found it impossible to refuse. Together, the two great statesmen who had just been planning the future and fate of a large portion of the world happily set out across the desert by motor car on the 150-mile journey to the romantic city. It was a five-hour drive, with thousands of U.S. troops strung out along the route and numerous airplanes circling vigilantly in the skies above it. *Commando* and the President's DC-4 were flown to an airstrip near the city. The leaders spent a convivial two days at a sumptuous private villa which had been placed at their disposal. With Churchill proudly and contentedly standing at his side, Roosevelt did sit in a chair in one of the villa's towers, and watch the sun set over the Atlas Mountains. He agreed with his enthusiastic colleague that it was, indeed, a magnificent sight. The two men, who had become such firm personal friends as well as allies, occasionally joined others in their party in a sing song. Sometimes Churchill sang a solo, with Roosevelt joining in the chorus. Once the president himself offered to give a solo performance but was interrupted by some incident or other before the assembly had a chance to make any critical appraisal of his vocal talent.

Whatever influence the conference might have had on the course of the war, it was obvious to Sir

Charles Wilson that the pleasant respite from their arduous duties in their respective capitals of Washington and London was having a decidedly beneficial psychological effect upon both Roosevelt and Churchill. On one occasion Harry Hopkins, the president's trusted aide, remarked to Churchill's physician, "The president came here because he wanted to make the trip; he is tired of sending me to London and Moscow. He loves the drama of a journey like this. They are always telling him that the president must not fly; it is too dangerous. This is his answer."

Certainly Churchill revelled in his release from the cares of 10 Downing Street and the endless political debates which droned along in the House of Commons, while Big Ben stroked off the late night hours over the rooftops of damp and chilly London in the full grip of winter. Sir Charles wrote:

> As for the P.M., when he gets away from his red (dispatch) boxes and leaves London, he puts his cares behind him. It is not only that he loves adventures; he feels, too, that he must "let up"; even a week or two away from the grind helps. He wants to shed for a little while, the feeling that there are more things to do in the twenty-four hours than possibly can be squeezed in. Perhaps Roosevelt has that feeling too. It is the instinct to escape, to take a long breath. Besides neither of them, in a way, has ever grown up.

When the time for the president to depart from Marrakech grew near, the two leaders said their formal farewells on the evening previous to the scheduled early morning takeoff of Roosevelt's aircraft. But, as the president's party was being loaded into cars for the trip to the airfield, a scuffing of slippers sounded on the stone floors of the Taylor villa and Churchill appeared, fresh out of bed and wearing one of his more spectacular dressing gowns, a flashy garment covered with brilliant red dragons. Clad only in this highly informal costume, the prime minister insisted on climbing into the car with the president and accompanying him not only to the airfield, but right into the waiting

DC-4 to make sure he was comfortably settled for the long and wearisome flight back to Washington.

Captain Vanderkloot, whose aircraft was parked not far away awaiting the bid of the prime minister, was standing near the ramp as Churchill, in his colorful garb, entered the aircraft with Roosevelt. Captain Otis Bryan, peering down from his window on the flight deck of the DC-4, turned startled eyes toward Vanderkloot. Captain Vanderkloot grinned and winked. He was quite accustomed to seeing the prime minister in such casual and sometimes dazzling attire. After all, it was almost his favorite kind of flying costume.

The prime minister, who usually appeared so casual and confident during his own distant and hazardous voyages in *Commando,* found it hard to restrain certain feelings of anxiety concerning the safety of the president as he prepared to set out that morning.

"These aeroplane journeys," Churchill later admitted, "had to be taken as a matter of course during the war. None the less I always regarded them as dangerous excursions."

Chapter Twenty

While the British cabinet back in London was so anxiously awaiting Churchill's return to the capital to give a full report in the House of Commons concerning the Casablanca Conference, the prime minister was mulling over entirely different plans. As he rested in Marrakech he was contemplating further voyages in *Commando* which did not include immediately returning to London, in spite of the urgent requests that he should do so. His plans involved another visit to Cairo and a flight to Turkey for discussions with President Inonu and other government leaders.

By this time the War Cabinet back in London was growing almost frantic over the far-ranging peregrinations of the prime minister, and was particularly worried about the risks involved in flying through so many areas where *Commando* might fall prey to roving enemy aircraft. The cabinet requested that he fly directly home from Marrakech without even returning to Cairo, let along making his proposed flight to Turkey. To which Churchill replied:

> The flight from Marrakech to Cairo has been carefully reconnoitred and considered, and is not thought to present any difficulties. It does not go over any enemy territory nor near any fighting fronts. The C.A.S. and the pilot think it a perfectly good and simple flight. The Chief of the Imperial General Staff and I need to go there in any case in order to discuss the whole question

with Wilson of his new command and the dispositions of the Tenth Army, on which we are now about to draw heavily for Sicily.

I trust that you and my colleagues will give me such latitude in my personal movements as I deem necessary to the public interest.

While Bill Vankerkloot and his crew stood with the big black Liberator near Marrakech, ready to carry out the wishes of "the Boss," Churchill, like some energetic schoolboy adventurer, was fretting over the restrictions his cabinet colleagues back in London were attempting to place upon him. Also, he was thinking affectionate thoughts about the trusty airplane which already had borne him safely across so many dangerous miles. He later wrote:

I got quite upset by the obstruction of the Cabinet as I lay in my luxurious bed in the Taylor Villa looking at the Atlas Mountains, over which I longed to leap in the 'Commando' airplane which awaited me so patient and contented on the airfield.

As usual, Churchill won the argument and the War Cabinet at last reluctantly withdrew its anxious request that he return forthwith to London. On the late afternoon of January 26 he was back aboard *Commando* heading for Cairo instead of London. This situation so appealed to his irrepressible and sometimes pranksome nature that he couldn't resist sending a brief and mocking message to Deputy Prime Minister Clement Attlee and Foreign Secretary Anthony Eden, trapped back in London's winter gloom. "We are just over the Atlas Mountains, which are gleaming with their sunlit snows. You can imagine how much I wish I were going to be with you tomorrow on the Bench, but duty calls."

When nightfall cloaked the lonely country as it unfolded beneath the strong wide wings of *Commando* following a compass heading eastward toward Cairo, Churchill retired once more to his bunk above the bomb bay:

I slept soundly till once again, after an eight months' interval, I went up to the co-pilot's seat and sat by Captain

Vanderkloot, my young American pilot, and we saw together for the second time dawn gleam upon the waters of the Nile. This time we had not to go so far to the south, because the victory of Alamein had swept our foes fifteen hundred miles farther to the west. We arrived at the airfield, ten miles from the Pyramids, and were welcomed by the Ambassador, Lord Killearn, and received by the Cairo Command.

As Bill Vanderkloot put the *Commando* into a shallow bank that morning and headed northward along the Nile on the final leg into Cairo, the "gleam upon the waters of the Nile" described by Churchill soon developed into the intense and almost blinding rays of the fully risen North African sun. To Vanderkloot's great embarrassment, the glare kept falling upon Churchill's eyes as he tried to study the terrain below. The curtain on the window beside the co-pilot's seat occupied by the prime minister was gathered in accordion pleats. It persisted in gradually sliding open again every time Vanderkloot reached over to pull it shut to block out the sun. Finally, in a desperate effort to preserve the comfort of his distinguished passenger, Bill Vanderkloot decided to keep the curtain shut with the only means at his disposal. Unsnapping the clasp which held the crisp new rose-colored ribbon of the Order of the British Empire to the breast of his tunic, he leaned over, pulled the curtain tight and secured it snugly with this pin.

A few moments later, Churchill realized what was holding closed the curtain that kept the sun out of his eyes. When he did recognize the pin, he peered at it closely, then turned to his pilot with a wide smile of pride and pleasure that seemed to Bill as radiant as the rising African sun. It had been a simple case of making do with what was available, to protect the prime minister from a temporary nuisance. But Churchill preferred to see special significance and symbolism in utilizing an O.B.E. ribbon to keep the sun out of the eyes of the leader of the Commonwealth and Empire. Obviously, he considered this an unusual gesture of respect indeed, from the captain of his aircraft. It helped to cement further a special kind of mutual respect and friendship between the British leader and young Bill Vanderkloot that endured after their wartime journeys, well into the postwar years.

Although Churchill enjoyed his visits to *Commando*'s flight deck and spent a great deal of time on it, there was scant opportunity for many conversations with the mighty voices of the four big Twin Wasps bellowing away steadily at cruising speed. Sometimes the prime minister sat there almost pensively, as though brooding on the vast and complex troubles and problems which had engulfed the world that lay far below the great wings of the aircraft. From almost two miles up, the earth upon which so many decisive struggles were being waged in so many places, could look deceivingly peaceful.

But there were times when Churchill arrived on the flight deck obviously in high spirits. Even the tip of his big cigar seemed to glow a little brighter on such occasions. Sliding into the co-pilot's seat beside Captain Vanderkloot, he would rub his hands together and declare, "I'm in fine fettle today!"

Always, this particular remark confirmed beyond all doubt that for the time being, at any rate, he was satisfied with the progress of the war. It also meant he was not exactly unhappy about the role he personally was playing, or planning to play, in the critical conflict then being waged on the land and the sea and in the air, on so many vastly scattered fronts.

On this particular trip Churchill informed Bill Vanderkloot that he intended to have *Commando* fly Field Marshal Smuts from Cairo to the United States, by way of London and Montreal. The prime minister regaled his pilot with yarns of his adventures during the South African War, and of how his old Boer enemy Smuts had become one of his closest friends and most respected advisors. Churchill, the man of action, plainly held the aging warrior and outstanding Empire statesman in high esteem.

"Treat him well, Vanderkloot, and guard his safety," said the prime minister. "He is a great asset to us."

After spending three days in Cairo conferring with British military and other officials concerning the progress of the North African campaign, Churchill once more took off in *Commando,* this time for the four-hour flight across the Mediterranean to Adana in Turkey. He arrived there on January 30, and spent the next two days talking with Turkish leaders in both the president's special train and a second one in which several saloon carriages had been put at the disposal of Churchill's party. In his discussions with the Turks, Churchill was joined by Sir Alexander Cadogan and General Sir Alan Brooke, Chief of the Imperial General Staff; General Sir Harold Alexander and General H. M. Wilson. Some of this party had flown to Adana in a second Liberator piloted by G. W. "Wendy" Reid, a Canadian member of R.A.F. Ferry Command who later was to have a long and distinguished career in Trans Canada Airlines and its successor, Air Canada. Of the Adana trip, Sir Charles Wilson recorded in his diary:

As we climbed into the aeroplane at Cairo, bound for somewhere in Turkey, we had a feeling that this particular trip was a little off the beaten track. Landing at Adana, where a number of cars met us, we drove through narrow, flat, muddy roads to a train in the siding. There was no platform, but we heaved the P.M. up into his compartment, and the train proceeded to meander along, at about eight miles an hour, under the shadow of the Taurus Mountains, until out of the snow-capped hills there crawled, 'like an enamel caterpillar', the President's train: I have borrowed this image from the P.M.; he likes it and has repeated it several times.

Our train pulled up with a great clanking of carriages in a siding. The President of Turkey descended from a compartment and climbed into our saloon, which had been prepared for luncheon. The President, his Prime Minister and his Foreign Minister are all deaf, and the Marshal who commands the Turkish Army, dour and aloof, may have been deaf too; he took so little part in the exchanges. On our side the P.M., the C.I.G.S. and Alex shouted cheerfully. Jumbo Wilson paired off with the Turkish Marshal, and no one feared that either would be guilty of any light indiscretions.

When Churchill and his party were preparing to take off from the small Adana airfield and depart from Turkey, Bill Vanderkloot and the crew of *Commando* suffered what was perhaps the greatest embarrassment of any in their jealously maintained efforts to look after the safety and comfort of "the Boss" at all times. The too efficient heater that gave Churchill the hotfoot on the way from London to Casablanca was bad enough. But the incident at Adana was really a blush-provoker, particularly for Captain Vanderkloot.

While taxiing out for the takeoff from the airfield, one of *Commando*'s big wheels strayed slightly off the edge of the runway and became securely bogged down in some unexpectedly soft ground. No matter how much Vanderkloot gunned *Commando*'s engines, the big Liberator refused to budge. It was finally necessary for Churchill to be debarked from the aircraft and taken aboard Wendy Reid's Liberator for the 45-minute flight to Cyprus. *Commando*'s crew was able to get her unstuck quickly enough to rejoin the party, shortly after it had arrived in Nicosia. But Wendy Reid had a lot of sport after this incident, needling Bill Vanderkloot about his famous passenger having to hitch a ride in the back-up plane. The event sorely distressed such a perfectionist as the youthful aviator whom Churchill by now had taken to calling affectionately, "my young American pilot."

Sir Charles Wilson wrote in his diaries the following description of how *Commando*, after finding her way safely through thousands of miles of perilous skies with her precious cargo, suffered the indignity of becoming stuck in the mud that day at Adana's small and rather primitive airport. The entry for January 31, 1973 read:

We slept in the train, and today the Turks came to lunch. Then the train returned as it came, at the same cautious pace, and the same cars took us to the same aerodrome, where the Turks had assembled in force to see us off. We bade friendly farewells and climbed into the big bomber. The engines roared and we began to move, and at that moment the pilot carelessly allowed the right wheel to leave the runway, whereupon the big tyre at once sank into the mud. The engines raced, but nothing happened. We were bogged. The Turks looked sympathetic. I was afraid that the P.M. might be upset by the delay, but when I looked around he was nowhere to be seen. I found him surrounded by Turks, who were all talking at once. Winston had taken charge in his best Sidney Street manner, and kept pointing at the wheel and gesticulating to the Turks. If only he could make them understand his plan.

(In his mention of "Sidney Street" Sir Charles was referring to the famed incident on that thoroughfare back in 1911 when Churchill, then serving as home secretary, had gone to the scene of action and personally directed the campaign being waged by soldiers and the London police to dislodge from a house a group of foreign anarchists who had barricaded themselves in the building and were holding a shoot-out with the forces of the law.)

"Lorries with chains appeared, but all was to no avail," wrote Sir Charles in his account of the misfortune at Adana. "The Turks crept away. Spades were produced and men dug around the sunken wheel. The P.M. removed his hat and mopped his head. At last it was decided we must change aeroplanes."

The rather testy reference of Sir Charles to *Commando*'s captain "carelessly" allowing one of the aircraft's wheels to stray off the narrow Adana airstrip would have done nothing to alleviate Vanderkloot's chagrin over the incident. But undoubtedly, it would have provoked some wry grins from the rest of *Commando*'s crew, who knew him to be one of the most assiduously careful and cautious pilots in the entire strength of Ferry Command.

Sir Charles wrote about the journey from Adana to Cyprus:

After the flight of less than an hour, we landed and drove to Government House, a comfortable mansion that had been built at the expense of the islanders in expiation of their crime in burning the old residency to the ground. Across the middle of the main reception room is a wooden partition, which, on pressing a button, rises slowly like a curtain and finally disappears into the ceiling. This new toy greatly intrigued Winston. Three times the performance had to be repeated, up and down. Tomorrow our bomber will take us back to Cairo.

On Cyprus, Churchill held a formal inspection of the 4th Hussars, of which he was honorary colonel. As the old war-horse passed between their ranks, he could sense from their expressions that the soldiers were receiving a great deal of satisfaction and pride from this special gesture, one which the prime minister probably enjoyed as much as anyone on the parade ground that day. On such an occasion he was a kind of walking, living banner for these fighting men so far from home.

While these ceremonies were taking place in Nicosia, *Commando*'s crew was busy making the big aircraft ready for the next leg of its journey. The Liberator was the object of a great deal of curiosity at the Nicosia airport as it sat there so large and mysterious, painted jet black instead of the more familiar mottled olive camouflage of most other R.A.F. machines. The identity of its famous passenger was known, and sightseers stayed back at a respectful distance outside the airport boundary fence as they stood gawking at the plane.

Inside, Radio Officer Russ Holmes proceeded to cook up some lunch for *Commando*'s crew on the small propane stove. Preparing precious bacon and fresh eggs that day, Holmes opened the astro hatch above the stove to expel the cooking odors as he whistled away at his chore. The pan grew quite hot while the bacon was frying and a spiral of smoke ascended from the opening in *Commando*'s roof. Suddenly there was a great wail of sirens and a frantic clanging of alarm bells as the Nicosia's airport fire truck came charging pell mell across the field. Someone, spotting the impressive smoke plume rising from *Commando*'s fuselage, had concluded that the aircraft was afire and had turned in an alarm.

At the end of his visit to Cyprus, Churchill and his

party once more boarded *Commando* for another flight to Cairo. The prime minister spent two nights in the Egyptian city. It had been expected earlier that after this second call at Cairo, *Commando* might be flying Churchill back to London, where his return was being awaited so impatiently by the War Cabinet and House of Commons.

But "the Boss" was not through yet with his energetic tour of the territory where the action was taking place. The flight plan now called for a continuation of the journey on to Tripoli, which had just been wrested from Rommel's Afrika Korps by the Eighth Army. By now *Commando*'s passengers included Churchill's son Randolph, who had come from the Tunisian front to join the prime minister. Sir Charles Wilson described in his diary the scene inside the cabin of the big aircraft as it steadily droned its way from Cairo westward across the desert:

> To Tripoli by air. The military situation here is full of problems. The C.I.G.S. (Field Marshal Sir Alan Brooke) sitting opposite me is, however, serenely indifferent to everything but Landsborough Thomson's *The Migration of Birds,* in which he has been immersed since we left the airfield at Cairo. The P.M., removing his cigar from his mouth, began advising Randolph to give up smoking. It made him cough for an hour every morning, leaving his voice husky, and as a politician his voice was part of his stock in trade; he was prejudicing his career for these wretched cigarettes. The plane was noisy and they were still bawling at each other as I fell asleep in my chair.
>
> When our bomber landed at Castel Benito, a lot of figures in khaki, fringing the airfield, rushed forward to greet the P.M. as he emerged in his Air Commodore's uniform. The P.M. advanced towards Monty and clasped his hand in both of his own. The Eighth Army had fought their way here hardly a fortnight ago, and now, in a grassy space, bounded by eucalyptus trees, the P.M. was in his element when he addressed the troops. No one can do this sort of thing so well.

Bill Vanderkloot and the rest of the crew couldn't resist some ironic grins when they surveyed the scene that spread before their eyes as *Commando* was taxied to the reception point for the prime minister. On *Commando*'s extremely brief and embarrassing visit to LG-224, the British had just left and the desert runways were virtually in German hands. Today it was obvious that, in this case, the *Germans* had just left this Tripoli field, and not very long before. The almost bewildering fluctuations in the fortunes of the highly mobile desert war were such that while the Union Jack flew proudly from its staff near where Churchill was greeting General Montgomery and other military chieftains, German anti-aircraft guns which seemed all ready for action were still scattered about the landing ground. A couple of disabled Luftwaffe fighter planes still stood in the field, with another resting in one of the hangars.

Churchill was plainly in "fine fettle" indeed as he briskly clambered down the steps of *Commando*'s ladder at the reception area. The prime minister and his party were taken aboard armoured cars and whisked off across the desert to the camp that served as a temporary British headquarters for the North African campaign.

Roaming about the desert airfield after *Commando* had been securely bedded down near a former Luftwaffe machine shop, the crew could see signs of the recent savage conflict all around them. Some portions of the runways were still badly pockmarked by explosions of bombs dropped by the R.A.F., a condition that had made it necessary for Vanderkloot to perform several cautious circuits of the field before setting the craft down to a landing. Bits and pieces of the debris of battle were everywhere. *Commando*'s crew even found a perfectly serviceable-looking German Mauser rifle protruding from some bushes. When they stopped to examine it, they could see a red wire running from the weapon back into the underbrush. Obtaining a long pole, the souvenir-hunters crouched behind some sandbags piled up nearby and gingerly fished the rifle out of the bushes, expecting a booby trap to explode at any moment. But it turned out that the piece of wire wasn't connected to anything and the rifle was carried back to *Commando* as booty of war.

Bill Vanderkloot and his crew were lodged in a building near the air base which had been used as a hospital during the German possession of the flying field. So hasty had been the departure of its former occupants that the operating rooms still looked as though they were ready for business at any moment. Bill Vanderkloot decided that, although the severe and antiseptic atmosphere of their quarters was not as luxurious as that in such places as Shepheard's Hotel, the rooms at least contained beds that looked as though he could sleep in one fairly soundly without scratching all night.

As they sat down in their hospital rooms that evening, *Commando*'s crew proudly examined their "short-snorter" bills to which had just been added, during the flight from Cairo, an illustrious new adornment in the form of the autograph of Winston Churchill. During the wartime days, those who had made long aerial journeys customarily carried a piece of paper currency which contained as many signatures as possible of distinguished persons with whom they had flown or whom they had met along the way. If the bearer of one short-snorter bill encountered the holder of another, he could challenge him to produce this glamorous certificate of trans-oceanic flights and if he didn't happen to be carrying it on his person, the careless victim of this ceremony was stuck for the drinks.

When the subject of short-snorters was brought up during the hop to Tripoli, Churchill was on *Commando*'s flight deck. He rather sheepishly explained that he was unable to produce at that very moment his own ten-shilling short-snorter note from the pocket of the dressing gown he so often wore during these visits to the co-pilot's seat. He did have it in a brief case back in the cabin, and hurriedly returned there to obtain it for the inspection of *Commando*'s crew. Technically, the prime minister was guilty of not having his bill actually on his person and therefore should have been stuck for drinks, or at least a pound or two in cash in lieu of the proper refreshments. However, it did not seem like a very good idea to Bill Vanderkloot and the rest of *Commando*'s crew to press the point, especially after Churchill had signed each of their own short-snorter bills with an appropriate flourish, while the big bomber roared through the night above the vastness of the Libyan Desert.

But, on the second day after their arrival at Tripoli, Churchill apparently had not ignored or forgotten completely after all, his obligations as a true member of the Order of the Short-Snorter. Much to Bill Vanderkloot's bewilderment, a British soldier appeared at the field hospital in an Army staff car at about 11 o'clock that night. He had been dispatched by the personal order of the prime minister to collect Captain Vanderkloot and drive him several miles to the field headquarters where Churchill was holding his meetings with the assembled military heads. Bill Vanderkloot naturally concluded that there had been some urgent and last-minute change in the prime minister's transportation plans and that he had been summoned in the middle of the night to discuss them.

But when he arrived at the tent where the meeting was taking place, he was greeted at the doorway by Churchill himself, wearing his familiar dark zip suit and puffing away happily on his great cigar.

"Do you have your short-snorter with you, Vanderkloot?" he asked.

Bill assured him that he did.

"Then come with me," said the prime minister, placing a reassuring hand on young Bill Vanderkloot's rather tense shoulder. "I've got a whole bag of prize autographs in here for you. Most of the entire British Imperial Staff, in fact, all in one bundle!"

Whereupon the greatly startled captain of *Commando* was presented to a most dazzling array of top British military brass that included: Generals Alexander and Montgomery; Air Marshal Arthur Tedder; Field Marshal Sir Alan F. Brooke, chief of the Imperial General Staff; General "Jumbo" Wilson; and Admiral of the Fleet Sir Andrew B. Cunningham. All dutifully signed Bill Vanderkloot's short-snorter note with a kind of dignity and aplomb they might have displayed affixing their signatures to a peace treaty with General Rommel.

As the young pilot from Lake Bluff, Illinois, was driven back to his quarters that night, under the sparkling desert stars, he concluded that "the Boss" was a remarkably human person indeed, to perform for the captain of his aircraft such a thoughtful gesture, especially in the middle of a conference with his renowned generals that concerned the whole course of the war in North Africa.

But Churchill, the master of the human touch as well as of the statesman's apt phrase and the determinedly·belligerent stance in the face of the foe, loved nothing better than the dramatic touch, whether it be the small matter of signing short-snorters for the captain of his aircraft or being on hand at a great turning point in history. It was little wonder, therefore, that he exuded such great confidence and satisfaction as he stood next day beside General Montgomery on the reviewing stand, while the Eighth Army made, as he put it, its "magnificent entry" into Tripoli, led by the pipers of the 51st Highland Division. In his address to the hard-bitten warriors who had so bravely and stubbornly recovered from defeat to drive Rommel's forces back across 1,500 miles of desert, he even quoted for them a couple of lines of poetry which seemed to particularly fit this victorious occasion:

"Yet nightly pitch our moving tent
A day's march nearer home."

Following his triumphant greeting to the Eighth Army from the side of its leader, General Montgomery, Churchill related to Bill Vanderkloot one of his favorite stories about the hero of El Alamein.

In 1942, Montgomery was having a discussion with Major-General Sir Hastings Ismay as they drove to the airport for Montgomery's hurried departure to North Africa immediately after he had been informed that he was to take over command of the battered and hard-pressed Eighth Army. Montgomery was lamenting the cruel lot of the professional soldier. He gave his whole life to his military career, devoting every possible hour to the study of his profession and rigorously developing the self discipline which would fit him for command. He toiled and made many personal sacrifices and hoped for advancement and recognition and finally, after years of effort, it seemed to come. He acquired a great command, won a great victory, and perhaps became world renowned. Then, in one foul stroke of fate—perhaps through no fault of his own—he encountered defeat and disaster and all of his life's work suddenly went down the drain.

At this point, the startled Ismay felt that the sorely depressed Montgomery needed a little bucking up. "You ought not to take this so badly," he said. "A very fine army is gathering in the Middle East. It may well be that you are not going to disaster."

"What!" cried the astonished Montgomery. "What do you mean? I was talking of Rommel!"

As he concluded his Tripoli visit, Churchill had in mind one more hop in *Commando* before ordering her to carry him back to London and his fretting colleagues in the British War Cabinet. On February 5, *Commando*, carrying Churchill and his party, thundered off the Tripoli airstrip and headed for Algiers, where the prime minister was to hold still another conference, with General Dwight D. Eisenhower and Admiral Cunningham.

At the end of the Algiers visit, Churchill was finally ready to return to London. But for awhile, it looked as though *Commando* wasn't. The starter on Number Four engine refused to function. Flight engineers Williams and Affleck were of that peculiar breed of Canadian flying men who believed that where there was a will there was usually a way. They coiled a length of rope around and around the propeller hub of Number Four engine, hooked it to a tractor, and went tearing off across the field, turning the propeller after the manner of a youngster spinning a top with a piece of string. Number Four responded with a mighty cough and then settled down to a contented purr that never faltered all the way back to London.

While all this was going on, Churchill was amusing himself by sitting in *Commando*'s cabin pretending to eye in very calculating fashion a particularly diminutive assistant secretary in his party. After closely looking the small chap over several times, the prime minister growled, "Your light weight is a great advantage in flying, but if we come down in the desert, you will not keep us going very long."

The direct flight from Algiers to London, however, was accomplished without further incident. There was no need to use the emergency rations to which the prime minister had so darkly and mischievously referred in his menacing remark to his startled secretary.

The big Liberator rolled to a stop right on the mark at Lyneham, where members of the British cabinet and other dignitaries had assembled to welcome the prime minister home from his long series of travels to Casablanca, Cairo, Tripoli, Adana, Cyprus and Algiers. Churchill paused, before departing from *Commando,* to favor Captain Vanderkloot with still another bit of constructive pilot-to-pilot criticism.

"That," said the prime minister, with a wide grin of satisfaction, "was the best landing you've made on the whole trip!"

Bill Vanderkloot tried to look suitably surprised and gratified by this expert opinion, secretly agreeing that it hadn't been such a bad demonstration at that, of what was known in the trade as "painting" the wheels of an airplane down to the surface of a runway.

Chapter Twenty-One

Prime Minister Churchill, with his constant thoughtfulness toward *Commando*'s crew and the kind of easy camaraderie he displayed toward them during his frequent visits to the flight deck, was by far their favorite passenger. But there were others whom the fliers discussed with considerable interest during the rag chews they sometimes held after special missions. In most cases, Captain Vanderkloot was too occupied with his duties on the flight deck to do much mingling back in the cabin with his passengers. He was able to make an occasional visit aft to carry out the normal courtesies displayed aloft by an aircraft skipper toward those dignitaries he was carrying aboard his plane. He inquired about their comfort and answered questions concerning *Commando*'s course, altitude and probable time of arrival at their destination. But such excursions were usually quite brief. In the case of Churchill, the big difference was that it was unnecessary to visit him often in his quarters back in the cabin because he was so frequently up on the flight deck visiting the crew.

None of *Commando*'s passengers, with the possible exception of Air Chief Marshal Portal, was more keenly enthusiastic about flying and the technical aspects of it all than the prime minister. On those occasions when he wore his air commodore's uniform, which he called his "disguise," he did so with obvious pride and satisfaction. After all, high flight through dangerous skies represented a special kind of adventure, and adventure had always been a vital part of Churchill's life, from the youthful days when he had ridden on what has been called the last great cavalry charge, in 1898, with the 21st Lancers at Omdurman, up through the years to his leadership of the British Commonwealth and Empire in its greatest time of trial. There was something particularly audacious about flying hither and yon under the very noses of the frustrated Luftwaffe that seemed to appeal greatly to his bold nature.

It is doubtful that any of *Commando*'s passengers ever had to stoop lower, upon mounting the ladder to pass through the comparatively small doorway to the aircraft's cabin, than Lord Halifax, British ambassador to Washington, when he was flown out to the United States from England. Bill Vanderkloot recalls that his lordship, a tremendously tall man, had about him a kind of funereal air, resembling that of some gaunt and lanky undertaker. But his stern appearance, *Commando*'s crew soon learned, was greatly deceiving. They were rather startled to discover that Halifax was a man of much wit and good humor, who had an easygoing and down-to-earth way of making conversation. This greatly endeared the man of such forbidding appearance to his colleagues in the Washington diplomatic community and made him one of the most popular British ambassadors ever to serve in the United States.

Dr. Wellington Koo, the Chinese ambassador to the Court of St. James, was a much more diminutive man who also provided a few surprises for *Commando*'s crew when they flew him across the Atlantic to take up his post in London. Perhaps because of the informal atmosphere that existed within such a vehicle as a converted bomber in flight across the ocean Dr. Koo was moved to favor *Commando*'s crew, during one visit to the flight deck, with a couple of solos on a traditional Chinese reed flute. He carried it with him on all of his travels and had developed an impressive amount of artistic skill. Its high, trilling notes were admirably complemented by the steady *basso profundo* of *Commando*'s great engines contentedly snoring away at cruising speed. The crew of the aircraft were so impressed by Dr. Koo's pleasant impromptu flute concert that they resolved they must pick up a couple of these melodious instruments the next time their global wanderings took them into the Far East.

Although *Commando* carried across the Atlantic such Canadian officials as Munitions and Supply Minister Clarence D. Howe, Minister of Defence J. L. Ralston and Lieutenant General Kenneth Stuart, Army Chief of Staff, they missed out on the opportunity of flying to Britain Prime Minister W. L. Mackenzie King on his maiden flight in an airplane. This assignment went to Captain L. V. Messenger, whose Ferry Command Liberator carried the prime minister from Dorval to Prestwick in August of 1941.

It was just as well because, according to eyewitnesses, Mr. King's emergence from the doorway of the big aircraft shortly after it rolled to a stop on the Prestwick tarmac lacked that certain dramatic dash more or less expected from national leaders when they arrive from afar to bring greetings to their fighting men. A large pipe band was assembled at the debarkation point, and as the Liberator came to a halt and stilled its motors the lively skirl of Scottish martial music and the thump of drums filled the misty air. An impressive honor guard of Canadian troops snapped to attention and several high officials stepped forward to greet the prime minister as the Liberator's door swung open. And then it happened. Somehow Mr. King, unaccustomed to disembarking from such aerial contraptions, managed to get stuck in the doorway while trying to emerge from it backwards.

"For what seemed like several minutes," a newspaperman who was on the scene later reported, "the dignitaries, the pipers and the honor guard that had been assembled for this historic moment, had to stand there staring at nothing else but the hind-end of the prime minister of Canada as he desperately tried to wriggle out of the doorway and down the ladder to terra firma. It certainly wasn't the kind of striking scene that might some day be immortalized on a postage stamp or prominently hung up in a war musuem!"

Among the numerous world figures carried at various times in *Commando* by Captain Vanderkloot and his crew, one, more than any of the others, was thought to be more critical cargo than even the heavy burden of ammunition carried in the aircraft from Accra to Tripoli. He was General Wladyslaw Sikorski, prime minister of Poland and commander in chief of the Free Polish forces. General Sikorski was what could only be called a "hard luck" airplane passenger—so much so, in fact, that there is still a great deal of speculation over whether he was the victim of plain misfortune or prolonged and dogged efforts by saboteurs acting in the interests of some power or powers determined to achieve his demise. His untimely death finally did take place, on July 4, 1943, when *Liberator* AL523, a sister ship of *Commando,* crashed into the sea moments after taking off from an airstrip in Gibraltar, killing Sikorski and all on board except the pilot.

Sikorski made three airborne visits to Canada and the United States during the war. On one, in March of 1942, a considerable furor was caused among the Allied intelligence agencies when, midway across the Atlantic, a Polish wing commander who was lying asleep in the bomb bay of the Liberator suddenly awakened to the smell of burning rubber. He extracted something from beneath the coats and blankets upon which he was reclining, and dashed to the toilet compartment of the aircraft. He later reported that he had discovered beneath the bedding a small bomb of a type used for the demolition of a force-landed aircraft likely to fall into enemy hands.

This incident was assumed to be an open-and-shut case of attempted sabotage of General Sikorski's aircraft. It might still have been regarded so to this day had not the wing commander finally confessed, after a great deal of investigation by British intelligence, that the bomb had actually belonged to him and that he had acquired it from a friend who worked on the production of such articles in Britain. He was expecting to go back on operations with the R.A.F. after the visit to the U.S. with Sikorski's party, he said, and intended to make use of the bomb if ever his aircraft were forced down in enemy territory. Why he insisted upon carrying it among his personal belongings on the trans-Atlantic trip, and why it had begun smouldering during the flight to Dorval, were questions which never seemed to be cleared up fully. The fact remains, however, that *Liberator AL523* narrowly missed going down into the Atlantic on that peculiar occasion.

A few months later, during Sikorski's flight with Vanderkloot in *Commando* from Prestwick to Washington by way of Gander and Dorval, a second mysterious incident took place. Upon his arrival at Dorval, after being flown across the Atlantic, the leader of the Polish Government in Exile was transferred to a smaller Hudson aircraft for the final leg of the trip to Washington. The flight from Prestwick had gone quite smoothly. But, just after the Hudson had taken off from Dorval, both engines faltered and lost power, making it necessary for the pilot to carry out a belly landing on what, fortunately, was a large enough area of clear ground beyond the end of the runway. No one was injured and the aircraft was not seriously damaged, but the exact cause of the engine failure remained a mystery.

The final misfortune of General Sikorski created the greatest mystery of all, to the extent that in recent years at least one play and one book have been written about it. The Liberator in which he, his daughter and other members of his party were setting out from Gibraltar enroute to London, took off shortly after 11 P.M. on July 4, 1943, with an experienced Czech pilot of R.A.F. Transport Command, named Flight Lieutenant Edward Max Prchal, at the controls. The aircraft made a normal takeoff, climbed to an altitude of about 200 feet and then went into a shallow dive down to a crash in the Mediterranean Sea, only about 700 yards out from the end of the runway.

Prchal, the only survivor, later testified at a court of inquiry held in Gibraltar that he had put the Liberator's nose down to gain some extra speed following the takeoff before beginning his climb to cruising altitude. The controls locked, forcing the aircraft to continue its shallow dive into the sea. Although the court of inquiry, in its findings, dismissed any possibility of sabotage, there is still no clear explanation of why the Liberator crashed so soon after takeoff.

Of all the hazardous areas traversed by *Commando* during her hundreds of thousands of miles in transporting high officials of the British and other governments to and from London or Montreal, the one that usually created the most anxiety for Captain Bill Vanderkloot and his four-man crew was the Bay of Biscay, lying between southern France and northern Spain. *Commando* skirted this part of the Atlantic Coast by wider and wider margins during repeated flights between London and North Africa by way of Gibraltar. But the rumors were that the Luftwaffe was modifying some of its fighter aircraft to extend their ranges farther out over the sea from their base near Biarritz, in southern France close to the Spanish border.

The German Intelligence Service appeared to know a lot more than the Allied Command hoped it would know about the special flights in which *Commando* carried, in addition to Prime Minister Churchill, various other war leaders on missions between Great Britain and the Middle East.

To down *Commando* during one of these special missions would have brought to a German fighter pilot so many high honors that even the Iron Cross would have seemed, by comparison, a mere consolation prize. During one of Churchill's journeys to the Middle East, William Joyce, the infamous "Lord Haw Haw" of Germany's propaganda radio broadcasts, was on the air within a few hours making the boast that the Nazi intelligence knew all about the Churchill's presence in Cairo. He reported that the Luftwaffe was preparing to put "a thousand planes in the air" to ensure that the prime minister would never return alive to England. But Churchill always managed to get back safely from these distant travels, and after the war, William Joyce ended up being sentenced in London's Old Bailey court room to death for treason.

On one occasion when Churchill was in the Middle East, German intelligence agents in Lisbon spotted a rather portly man, smoking a large cigar and wearing sunglasses, boarding a commercial airliner about to proceed from neutral Portugal to Britain. Jumping to the rather ridiculous conclusion that this mysterious passenger was Churchill attempting to return incognito to London on a regular airline flight, the Nazi spies flashed the word to Berlin. Shortly after the airliner's takeoff from Lisbon the helpless craft was shot down somewhere over the Bay of Biscay, probably by Me-109s from the Biarritz Luftwaffe base. All aboard were killed, one of the victims of this outrage being British actor Leslie Howard.

Small wonder, then, that the neighborhood of the Bay of Biscay was considered to be such a highly dangerous area during *Commando*'s fairly frequent flights between London and the Middle East. It was on this leg of two different journeys that Bill Vanderkloot received what he later admitted were his greatest scares while flying Allied war leaders. In both incidents, Field Marshal Jan Christiaan Smuts, prime minister of South Africa, was *Commando*'s distinguished passenger.

On the first flight with Smuts, the London-bound *Commando* was flying in the vicinity of the Bay of Biscay when radio operator Russ Holmes released a length of wire which, after being unreeled, trailed out from the aircraft's tail section to provide an antenna. The wire was dragged out and kept in a fairly horizontal position by a small metal cone, called the "fish," which was attached to the end of it. It so happened that on this particular day, flight engineer Ron Williams was tinkering back in the tail section when the antenna was released. He sat there for a few moments idly watching through the transparent tail turret the lively and erratic movements of the fish as it dipped and dived in the slipstream at the end of the antenna. Beside him was *Commando*'s 50 m.m. tail gun which Captain Vanderkloot fervently hoped would never have to be fired in anger.

The more Williams studied the peculiar movements of the fish on the end of the antenna, the more it appealed to him as an ideal make-believe target for the sights of *Commando*'s solitary tail gun. After all, he figured, practice makes perfect, and one never knew when a bit of perfect shooting might be required to preserve the lives of *Commando* and all those aboard her. He gripped the gun firmly and began to follow the movements of the frisky fish as it darted about behind the aircraft. Then a peculiar and immensely embarrassing thing happened. Although Williams had not the slightest thought of actually firing the gun, he somehow placed just a little too much pressure on the trigger during one swing of the weapon and a sudden burst of shots poured out of the cannon.

Up on *Commando*'s flight deck, Bill Vanderkloot and co-pilot Jack Ruggles jumped so high off their seats that their heads almost hit the ceiling. They were certain that the moment of truth had finally arrived, over the Bay of Biscay, and that the next gunfire heard would be that of a Messerschmitt-109 as its bullets tore through *Commando* from stem to stern. Vanderkloot hastily turned the controls over to Ruggles and went racing back toward the tail section to see what Williams was shooting at. He met his red-faced engineer about half way along the route, scrambling toward the flight deck to assure the rest of the crew that the whole thing had been a ghastly mistake and all was well.

The one person aboard who seemed to be least perturbed was Prime Minister Smuts, who merely nodded nonchalantly when informed that the firing of *Commando*'s cannon was only a routine test and that the weapon had been found to be in perfectly good working order.

But the next alarm aboard *Commando,* a few months later, as she droned her way northward high over the Atlantic, in the same dangerous area along the outskirts of the Bay of Biscay, was no such laughing matter. The moment of stark and grim reality brought a sudden and chilling materialization of the vague, disturbing nightmares which had haunted every member of *Commando*'s crew, during their tense months of flying to and from the distant places so many important figures in the Allied war effort. It came on a quite pleasant day while *Commando* was again making her way from Gibraltar to London, enroute from Cairo to North America and once more carrying Field Marshal Smuts.

Down under *Commando*'s wings lay scattered cloud layers at about 6,000 feet, and below them spread the wide blue expanse of a fairly calm sea, rolling toward the northern coast of Portugal. Soon, *Commando* would be flying not far westward of the entrance to the Bay of Biscay, and after that always hazardous stretch had been traversed, it would not be long before there came the welcome and familiar landfall on the south coast of England.

Back in the cabin, the South African prime minister and his aides were sipping fresh cups of hot tea which had just been brewed on *Commando*'s propane stove by radio operator Russ Holmes. Up on the flight deck, engineer Ron Williams was checking *Commando*'s fuel consumption while Vanderkloot and Ruggles estimated their position on an aerial map spread out upon the co-pilot's knees. Outside, the four big Wasps were humming away smoothly as they contentedly bit off the last miles to England, aided by a helpful quartering tailwind.

Ron Williams rose from his seat before the instrument panel, which was conveying to his watchful eye the highly satisfactory state of health of *Commando*'s power plants, and glanced idly out through a window on the starboard side. Suddenly he froze for a moment. Then he slammed a hand on Vanderkloot's shoulder.

"Hey!" he cried. "Take a look over there skipper, at about two o'clock! Two Me-109s, heading this way at a hell of a rate!"

Vanderkloot and Ruggles peered through the cockpit windshield. There was no doubt about it. They were Messerschmitts, all right, closing the gap which lay between them and *Commando* at a horrifying rate. This was the kind of moment that Bill Vanderkloot had always thought would have to come, sooner or later. Now it was here and there wasn't a chance in the world that *Commando*'s pitifully meager armament could effectively defend her from the guns of the speedily approaching German fighters.

Dead ahead, and about two thousand feet below, lay a fairly heavy cloud layer. Toward it Bill Vanderkloot dived the big black Liberator with engines all out at full throttle, and at such a steep angle of descent that the wind shrieked like an angry banshee around her wings and fuselage, and her controls vibrated violently. In only split seconds, the enemy aircraft would be within shooting range. The difference between life and death for *Commando,* for the renowned Empire statesman she was carrying and for all the rest of her passengers and crew now delicately teetered upon a few agonizing moments which were being so relentlessly ticked off by the sweep hand on the dashboard clock. At any time now the staccato clatter of shells ripping through *Commando*'s fuselage could mark the end of the seemingly charmed life she had lived for so long.

Then, abruptly, like the soft and sheltering wings of some guardian angel, the first thin whisps at the edge of that cloud bank hanging over the Bay of Biscay began to enshroud *Commando*. Moments later her very wingtips had disappeared from the view of those on her flight deck as she flew through a strange, dim world where even her four great Wasp engines became more muted in their throaty song. Once more the carefully honed weapons of stealth and evasiveness— plus a bucketful of luck—had been more effective than guns in preserving *Commando* on her high and lonely errands.

Having gained the protection of the cloud layer, Vanderkloot quickly altered *Commando*'s compass heading by ninety degrees and flew westward straight out into the Atlantic, holding this course until he was certain he was far beyond range of the Biarritz Luftwaffe base, before turning northward once more toward England.

When *Commando* finally emerged into clear skies again, the wide and beautiful expanse of blue over the Atlantic was once more free of menace. But it had been an extremely narrow squeak. Had the cloud layer where *Commando* took refuge been only a few miles farther away when the Me-109s were sighted, the big Liberator almost certainly would have gone down before their guns.

Throughout the whole frightening incident there was no one aboard *Commando* who remained more calm than Field Marshal Smuts. He was a most remarkable man. From his weatherbeaten face, with its neatly trimmed beard, there shone cold, grey-blue eyes which focused their penetrating gaze from above prominent cheek bones. He was said by some of his associates to seem remote even from his own South African people and the members of his cabinet. Carrying with him at all times his Greek Testament, he was an austere man who sometimes lived in a private world of his own. Yet the crew of *Commando* found themselves greatly liking and respecting the reserved and dignified old warrior whom they ranked right next to Churchill as their favorite passenger. Like Churchill, he displayed an extremely keen interest in all aspects of flying and took a great deal of pleasure out of making occasional visits to the flight deck.

As *Commando* continued northward toward England, Bill Vanderkloot found himself sitting at the controls, meditating upon the strange tricks which fickle chance could play, and wondering just how long luck could continue to hold out for the aircraft that had become so famous not only among Allied airmen, but among the pilots of the Axis air forces as well.

Never had he had any aspirations to be a fighter pilot or a bomber pilot. His main ambition, he had once frankly admitted, was to become an "old, safe pilot." Not for him the triumphant victory rolls in a

Spitfire or a Mustang or the satisfaction of seeing a bomb pattern land dead on target.

"The idea of killing other people, or being killed myself, never did appeal to me much," he confessed. "You might say I was a sissy in this respect, completely dedicated to a basic desire to protect my own skin and that of my passengers in every possible way."

To that object he had devoted all of his time and had constantly sharpened all of his skills as a pilot. One possibility that particularly disturbed Bill Vanderkloot was that he was almost certainly marked for close personal observation by enemy agents working within Britain. He sensed that his movements in London and perhaps even in Montreal were being followed carefully, because any preparations he might make for a new mission nearly always signalled an aerial journey by some important Allied leader. The Air Ministry indicated it was entertaining similar misgivings, by applying to him the pseudonym of "Wing Commander Jones" when communicating with him concerning upcoming missions.

Chapter Twenty-Two

During the early months of 1945, a peculiar mood began to develop on *Commando's* flight deck amongst the normally lighthearted team of young men who had gone through so many adventures together in the air, who had happily roamed the streets of curious and far-off places, and who had enjoyed so many convivial occasions with each other and their families back in the snug haven of Montreal between missions in the big Liberator. It was a change of attitude so subtle that it probably would never have been noticed by others, even those who knew them well. But it was there, all right, plain enough to be sensed ever so vaguely, by this tightly-knit little group who had worked and played together for more than two years. Just as they were so finely tuned to the most minute change in the sound and feel of *Commando,* they were keenly sensitive to the moods of each other.

Tension. There was always tension, of course, while guiding *Commando* along those dangerous and potentially treacherous pathways in the sky which she was called upon to follow while transporting Allied leaders on urgent missions of various kinds, missions which the enemy would so dearly have loved to see end in disaster. But gradually it was growing more acute. The tensions involved in such aerial journeys could only be fully realized by those who were familiar with the fantastic security measures which surrounded the movements of high-ranking Allied officials during their wartime travels in other vehicles of various kinds. When Prime Minister Churchill made one journey to the United States aboard the Queen Mary, for example, all sorts of elaborate ruses were used in an attempt to disguise the fact that he was being carried across the Atlantic on the great liner. At one point, before its departure from the Clyde, notices written in Dutch were posted in various parts of the ship to give the impression that it was about to carry Queen Wilhelmina and her suite to North America. Then, in an effort to further confuse enemy intelligence agents, ramps were ostentatiously constructed in the passages of the Queen Mary in the hope of starting a rumour that the liner was making the trip to the United States to bring back President Roosevelt.

When *Commando* was carrying some important personage, however, the ways in which the nature of the mission could be disguised were comparatively limited. The activities of such a journey, being concentrated basically into the movements of a five-man aircrew and the persons their aircraft carried, didn't leave much room to contrive any great degree of elaborate deception. So far as trips to the Middle East were concerned, the handy German observation tower across the fence from Gibraltar airport was, in itself, a highly frustrating factor in trying to keep secret from enemy agents the exact nature of *Commando*'s missions. This factor was particularly disturbing in view of the refueling stops at the British fortress, necessary during trips to points such as Cairo.

Then there was the stark remaining fact that as soon as *Commando* took to the air, she was entirely and almost helplessly alone. A chance meeting with just one lucky Luftwaffe fighter plane probably would spell her doom. This hard truth was always difficult to dispel completely from the minds of those who manned her flight deck.

The situation created a growing psychological problem that began to trouble Bill Vanderkloot more frequently as the months passed by. His uneasy thoughts dwelt not only on the safety of himself and his crew, but on that of the various important officials they were called upon to fly in *Commando*. Vanderkloot began to dread more often that some slight accidental slip of his own might allow enemy agents to gain the information that would open the way to tragedy while he flew Churchill or some other personage. The heavy mental pressure that was always present whenever *Commando* was in the air on a special mission now began to exert itself even on the ground between trips, so there was little respite in Vanderkloot's anxiety. Some peculiar sixth sense, which had served him so well while guiding *Commando* on many thousands of miles of hazardous travels, now seemed to be telling him that time was running out and his previously abundant share of luck was becoming exhausted. He began to lose weight and found it increasingly difficult to relax even at home in Montreal with Della and Patricia.

Della, who had helped console so many new widows in the Tower Apartments when crushing news suddenly arrived in the households of her neighbors, had always taken great pains to conceal her own anxieties during those brief periods when Bill Vanderkloot was able to be at home again with his family. Whenever he bade her goodbye to leave upon still another mission to some far-off corner of the world, they tried to treat these partings in fairly casual manner. But always, as he left her at the door or climbed from their car after she had driven him out to the airport at Dorval, they shared uneasy thoughts which they knew were better left unexpressed. Sometimes, at the airport, Della stood beside the car for a long time, watching *Commando* roar down the runway, climb into the sky and gradually shrink to a lone and tiny speck that finally became lost beyond the eastern horizon. She too was beginning to feel more and more the burden of this increasing strain—perhaps more than Bill Vanderkloot himself. After all, it was one thing to be busily occupied with the many chores involved in carrying out such critical flying missions and quite another to merely sit at home and wait. But whenever

Bill mentioned his thoughts about giving up his special duties, Della did her best to conceal her own feelings in the matter. That was the way it had to be with all the wives in that closely-knit community of airmen who plied their risky trade from Dorval in those dangerous wartime days.

One night at Prestwick, at the conclusion of a flight from Montreal, Bill Vanderkloot discussed with Jack Ruggles and the other members of his crew the possibility of asking for a transfer to different duties. By then they had flown *Commando* safely almost 200,000 miles, mostly on special missions. They had carried more high ranking personages than any other aircraft in the R.A.F. During all of this time, not one passenger had been harmed nor had *Commando* received a scratch. It was a remarkable record, considering the growing attention the aircraft had been receiving for many months from the German intelligence service and the Luftwaffe. By this time enemy agents were frequently and closely watching the movements of at least some members of the crew, if not all of them. Certainly there had been enough newspaper photographs of them published to make their faces familiar to those who had a special interest in identifying them. The chances were becoming greater, after every special flight, that the efforts of the enemy intelligence would eventually pay off, either by the sabotage of *Commando* or an attack in the air. The odds against such a happening were becoming slimmer with each passing day. The encounter with the two Me-109s, so far out to sea on the edge of the Bay of Biscay, could hardly have been a pure coincidence. Obviously, at such an unusual distance from their base, they had been hunting for very big game, and had nearly bagged it. Next time the luck might be on their side, rather than *Commando*'s. *Commando* had had more than her share of good fortune. Perhaps it was time to recognize the fact. The same instincts of caution which had allowed *Commando*'s crew to chalk up such a superb record were at last saying that the percentages in this grim game of chance were no longer working in their favor.

And so it was agreed that night that they would ask for a transfer.

Their request was reluctantly granted by the Air Ministry, and the crew of *Commando* took up other and more routine duties in the organization, by now known as R.A.F. Transport Command, which was becoming a kind of worldwide military airline operation as well as a means of ferrying aircraft to the various theatres of war.

Commando was taken over by another R.A.F. crew under Wing Commander "Willie" Biddell, O/C of No. 231 Transport Squadron, based at Dorval.

* * *

On March 28, 1945, shortly after the former crew of *Commando* had relinquished their special duties, Prime Minister Churchill sadly rose in the House of Commons to make a grave announcement. As he looked around the chamber and began to speak, there was a tremble of emotion in his voice that could be clearly detected by his fellow members of Parliament. He informed the House that, while on a flight the previous day from London to Canada, during which Wing Commander Biddell had been carrying a group of high Air Ministry officials including Sir John Abraham, deputy undersecretary of the Air Ministry, and Air Marshal Sir Peter Drummond, *Commando* had been lost with all aboard, in the vicinity of the Azores, in the Atlantic. Only a few bits of floating debris were found by the British destroyers which searched the area, but indications were that *Commando* had been lost as a result of enemy action, involving either sabotage or an aerial attack while in flight over the Atlantic.

* * *

Near the end of 1945, Bill Vanderkloot left the service to return to the United States, where he had accepted a position as chief pilot for a large industrial corporation. When he took off his dark blue uniform jacket of the R.A.F. Transport Command for the last time, it bore upon its breast, in addition to the O.B.E., the ribbon of an honorary commander of the Order of the British Empire, one step below the rank of knighthood and the highest award of its kind that could be bestowed by a grateful British king upon an American civilian pilot.

EPILOGUE

March, 1946

Arriving one day at the Long Island airfield near Manhasset where he was operating as chief pilot for a U.S. industrial concern, Captain Bill Vanderkloot was informed by a blasé and incredulous telephone operator that some "nut" who claimed he was calling on behalf of Winston Churchill in New York had been trying to obtain his home number. Of course, she had refused to give it out to him, in accordance with company rules in matters of this kind. She had agreed, however, to take the telephone number of this obvious prankster and had promised to give Vanderkloot the message upon his return to the office.

Vanderkloot immediately called the number, which turned out to be that of the Waldorf Astoria, and was put through to a suite in the Towers. In a few moments he was listening to the unforgettable voice of his favorite wartime passenger, greeting him in extremely warm and hearty fashion. Could Vanderkloot come to dinner with him and Mrs. Churchill on the following evening? The rather astonished Vanderkloot managed to stutter out that he would indeed be delighted.

The dinner turned out to be a most remarkably informal affair. It was served not in one of the hotel's dining rooms, but right in the suite, after being prepared in the small kitchen by Mrs. Churchill her-

self. At the end of this homey repast, the British statesman invited Vanderkloot to join him in the drawing
room, where they sat for some hours, talking of old
times aboard *Commando* and about her historic missions on behalf of the prime minister and other wartime leaders.

As Vanderkloot rose to leave that evening, Churchill asked him to wait for a few moments.

"You must take something along to mark this
happy occasion," he said.

He then went rooting about his baggage in the
suite and finally emerged from a bedroom carrying
with him a rather dog-eared volume of one of his early
books, published in 1932 and titled *Amid These Storms,
Thoughts and Adventures, by the author of A Roving Commission.* On the dust jacket was a photograph of a much
more youthful Winston Churchill, wearing a battle hel-
met and military greatcoat.

Taking out his pen, Churchill wrote in the fly leaf,
"To William Vanderkloot, from his friend Winston
Churchill, with buoyant memories of 'Commando'.
May she rest in peace."

They shook hands that evening, in the doorway of
the suite in the Waldorf Towers, and that was the last
time Bill Vanderkloot saw the great statesman with
whom he had shared so many days and nights of high
adventure.

*　　*　　*

March, 1971

During a routine flying errand for his company,
Bill Vanderkloot had landed his aircraft on a small airfield in Oklahoma near the Texas border and was busy
overseeing the job of making it secure for the approaching night, when a small car drew up to the roadside near the fence. The driver, after studying the trim
French-made Falcon jet for awhile, climbed out of his
car and came over to where Vanderkloot was standing
beside his plane.

The stranger, speaking with a pronounced German accent, explained that during the war he had

been an aircraft pilot himself, in the Luftwaffe, and asked whether Bill Vanderkloot would mind his having a closer look at his machine because it was the first one of its type he had seen. After they had exchanged introductions, Vanderkloot showed the visitor about the aircraft while, pilot to pilot, they discussed its various features.

As he was about to leave, the stranger said, "Vanderkloot.... Vanderkloot.... It is a name that was quite familiar to me in the wartime days, but I don't imagine you could possibly be the same one.... There was this Vanderkloot who flew Churchill and other war leaders between England and the Middle East, and many times, when I was stationed in Biarritz, my comrades and I roved the sky far and wide over the Bay of Biscay, hoping to some day get a shot at him, when our intelligence had told us he might be heading our way."

Bill Vanderkloot assured the astonished visitor that he was indeed the pilot he had in mind, and for a few moments the two old enemies stood eyeing each other in shocked disbelief that chance should finally bring about this strange meeting by a country roadside, in Oklahoma.

A few weeks after this curious incident, Bill Vanderkloot received the following letter, signed by Major Von Clough:

My Dear Captain:

Our last meeting was on a small field in southeastern Oklahoma.... I hope that God has been looking over you as well as He has over myself and as He did that day our vectors did not meet out of Portugal. It has always been my belief that He does smile just a little more upon the men who fly more closely to Him and we who so often rely upon His guidance when all else fails. This, too, creates a comradeship among pilots, one to the other, even though they may come from the ends of the earth.

Strange how fate brought us together in Oklahoma and kept us apart so many years ago, which surely shows an intent was there that we were destined to know each other well in mutual friendship and co-operation, working together.

199

I shall close this letter to you with a statement from a small Arab boy who touched my life but briefly. I had force landed and jerry-rigged my malfunctions and was just about to pull her out when he leaned over to me and said: "May Allah lift your feet."

I firmly believe that that one extra prayer gave me the mite more clearance I needed!

My compliments, Captain, and may Allah always lift your feet.

*   *   *

July, 1971

While flying some company executives to Newfoundland, where the firm had mining interests, Bill Vanderkloot found himself landing once more at Gander Airport, the scene of so many earlier adventures, hilarious evenings, marathon poker games, long hard and anxious looks at the brooding eastern skies extending far out over the Atlantic, and—all too often—the stunning impact of sudden tragedy.

There is a small cemetery situated on a hill quite close to the airport, where lie a number of Bill Vanderkloot's old comrades of Ferry Command, killed while approaching or leaving that terminal. He walked up there one day during his stay at Gander and stood for a long time, amid the humble markers over the graves of the friends with whom he had shared so many dangers and moments of triumph in the long ago days. The North Atlantic then had seemed so much broader and more menacing to those who pioneered the high pathways in the sky now followed by larger, speedier and marvelously instrumented aircraft, in such routine manner.

By now, the wild native grass had almost overrun this small cemetery. The green blades stood knee-high, waving in the restless winds from the Atlantic. Not far down the slope, some kind of garbage dump had been established, piled with old cardboard cartons, rusty tin cans, discarded bedsprings, and similar refuse.

Very slowly and sadly, Bill Vanderkloot walked back down that lonely hill, surrounded by his memories and the vast Newfoundland wilderness.

"There wasn't a monument of any kind up on that forlorn and forgotten little hill for all those great fellows," he later recalled. "Just those weatherbeaten little markers, almost covered by the grass . . . . It just didn't seem right . . . . But I guess that's the way things sometimes are, after a war, when the job is finished and the loud cheers have all died down."

Trans-Atlantic airliners originally had followed through Gander the trail that had been blazed so well by such adventurous men as those buried on that bleak Newfoundland hill. Now they spurned the island that had figured so often throughout the years in man's bold aerial challenge and conquest of the wide sea that separated the Old World from the New.

They flew high and fast and aloof and almost disdainfully above the broad North Atlantic, beyond and over Newfoundland, directly to their destinations from bustling terminals on the North American mainland. There are said to be computers in New York and Montreal which can tell you almost exactly at what altitude and rate of progress each of these machines is flying at any minute of the day or night. But there is as yet no way of programming into these marvelous flickering boxes the factors of the past—the fears, the hopes, the courage, the triumphs, the heart-breaking disappointments and the stark tragedies—which brought about the now so casually-accepted miracle of traversing, with such great ease and confidence, those forever cruel and surly seas.

The End